Table of Contents

Additional Resources

Illuminating Universals

Catholic Insights into the Structures of Existence

by

Dr. ant

No part of this book may be reproduced in any form or by any electronic or mechanical means including information storage and retrieval systems, without permission in writing from the author. The only exception is by a reviewer, who may quote short excerpts in a review.

Although the author and publisher have made every effort to ensure that the information in this book was correct at press time, the author and publisher do not assume and hereby disclaim any liability to any party for any loss, damage, or disruption caused by errors or omissions, whether such errors or omissions result from negligence, accident, or any other cause.

This publication is designed to provide accurate and authoritative information with regard to the subject matter covered. It is sold with the understanding that the publisher is not engaged in rendering professional services. If legal advice or other expert assistance is required, the services of a competent professional should be sought.

The fact that an organization or website is referred to in this work as a citation and/or a potential source of further information does not mean that the author or the publisher endorses the information the organization or website may provide or recommendations it may make.

Please remember that Internet websites listed in this work may have changed or disappeared between when this work was written and when it is read.

Illuminating Universals: Catholic Insights into the Structures of Existence

Contents

Glossary of Terms

Additional Resources

Introduction

The pursuit of truth has driven humanity across millennia, from the earliest philosophical inquiries to the complex queries of modern science. We are innately drawn to seek answers, to understand the universe, to comprehend our place within it, and to decipher the force that orchestrates this intricate symphony of existence. This book, in its essence, seeks to guide you—a Roman Catholic, a university professor, a scientist, a skeptic, a philosopher, and a mathematician—through a profound exploration that ultimately exalts the Roman Catholic Church as the living manifestation of divine purpose and design.

Our journey begins with recognition of the enduring quest for understanding that unites us all. Whether driven by faith or reason, or perhaps a synthesis of both, we find ourselves at a crossroads of disciplines. At this intersection, the Roman Catholic Church stands not only as a bastion of spiritual guidance but also as a repository of centuries-old wisdom that integrates theological insights with the empirical rigor of science and philosophy.

Imagine the universe as an elaborate puzzle, each piece interlocking with others to reveal a grand design. From the elemental laws governing the cosmos to the intricacies of biological systems, and from the abstract elegance of mathematical theorems to the profound depths of philosophical inquiry, there exists a unifying thread—a divine blueprint that points unmistakably to an intelligent creator. This introduction serves as a prologue to a compendium that elucidates this intricate tapestry, demonstrating that the convergence of all universal truths leads inexorably to the Roman Catholic Church.

Throughout recorded history, human civilization has observed patterns in the natural world and sought to understand their significance. Ancient scholars, theologians, and scientists alike have contributed to an ever-expanding repository of knowledge. We shall delve into historical perspectives, observing how universal structures have been identified across various disciplines. These structures are not mere coincidences but are markers of divine intelligence, guiding us toward deeper understanding and faith.

The chapters that follow are meticulously curated to bring forth evidence of this divine order, presented through the lens of different fields of study. For instance, the liturgical calendar of the Roman Catholic Church, with its key seasons and feasts, is more than a spiritual tool—it is a reflection of cosmic and symbolic significance. The intricate design manifests itself not only in religious observances but also in the periodic table of elements, where the foundational principles and cosmic arrangements reveal a divine symphony woven into the very fabric of matter.

Consider the human body, a marvel of integrated systems that showcases both spiritual and biological interconnectedness. Each heartbeat, each breath, and every neural impulse speak of an intelligent design that transcends mere biological function. Similarly, as we explore the fundamental forces and elements of the universe, we shall discover the theological implications embedded within cosmology, pointing to a creator whose craft is evident in every quark and galaxy.

In the realm of mathematics, the universals that govern equations and theorems are reflections of divine order. These core principles, universally accepted and endlessly applicable, validate the presence of an overarching intelligence. The patterns and consistencies in scientific theorems and laws further highlight the invisible hand of the creator, steering the natural world with precision and grace.

Philosophical discourse, too, serves as a bridge between faith and reason. Throughout history, key philosophical concepts have been woven into arguments for a divine architect. These intellectual pursuits enrich our understanding, presenting a coherent narrative that aligns scientific inquiry with theological doctrine. In doing so, they challenge both believers and skeptics to consider the harmonious design behind existence.

A comparative analysis of structural concepts across various domains will reveal remarkable similarities, underscoring the impact of these universals on human understanding. The concurrent exploration of faith and reason will illustrate how these seemingly disparate threads are, in truth, intertwined strands of the same divine tapestry. The Roman Catholic Church, with its rich tradition of intellectual and spiritual inquiry, offers a unique vantage point from which to appreciate and interpret these truths.

Faith and reason, often presented as opposing forces, find harmony within the teachings of the Church. This synthesis is crucial in understanding the universe and our place within it. By harmonizing science and religion, we can appreciate the full spectrum of human knowledge, from empirical evidence to spiritual wisdom. The chapters ahead will delve into this intricate dance, shedding light on the evidence of intelligent design and its implications for believers and skeptics alike.

The ultimate goal of this book is to lead all into God's Roman Catholic Church by presenting proofs of divine origin evident in the natural and intellectual worlds. These proofs are not confined to theological discussions but are manifested in the very structure of reality. The universal call to the Roman Catholic Church resonates through the cosmos, inviting all to witness the harmonious design that underscores our existence.

In conclusion, this introduction serves as a gateway to a comprehensive exploration of the universal truths that lead to the exaltation of the Roman Catholic Church. As we journey through the subsequent chapters, may we open our hearts and minds to the wonder of divine design, recognizing the intricate interplay of faith and reason that points us toward a greater understanding of our creator. Let this book be a testament to the timeless pursuit of truth, a journey that transcends disciplines and unites us all in the quest for divine wisdom.

The path ahead is one of discovery and revelation. Welcome to a journey that seeks to bridge the gap between empirical evidence and spiritual enlightenment, guiding us toward the recognition of the Roman Catholic Church as God's ordained institution. Through the exploration of divine blueprints, liturgical significance, cosmic arrangements, biological marvels, mathematical universals, and philosophical truths, we shall uncover the undeniable reality of a creator whose ultimate desire is to draw all creation into His embrace.

Chapter 1: The Divine Blueprint

The concept of a divine blueprint implies an underlying, intricate design orchestrated by a higher power. This chapter delves into the nature of that design, compellingly arguing that the universe and everything within it is not a chaotic accident, but a meticulously planned creation. The Roman Catholic Church emerges as the key holder of this divine plan, offering a path to understanding the ultimate purpose and meaning behind our existence.

From the grand architecture of galaxies down to the minute details of cellular structures, historical perspectives provide a rich tapestry illustrating God's hand in everything. Ancient civilizations often gazed at the heavens and saw not just stars but divine messages. They built great monuments like the pyramids and cathedrals, each with precise alignments and proportions, reflecting their quest to synchronize with the cosmic order. These historical insights lay the foundation for us to appreciate a universe designed with intention, where Roman Catholicism holds a vital role in interpreting this divine blueprint.

Universal structures and patterns manifest across various disciplines, serving as a testament to the coherent and intelligent design by the Creator. For instance, mathematical ratios and fractals are evident in nature, art, and architecture. Consider the Fibonacci sequence, which appears in pinecones, seashells, and even the human body. These patterns are more than coincidences; they reveal a master plan encoded into the very fabric of our existence. It is within the Roman Catholic Church that we find the theological and philosophical keys to unlocking this profound reality.

Philosophers and scientists alike have sought to understand the principles guiding our universe. From Plato's ideal forms to Einstein's theories of relativity, these intellectual pursuits reveal a universe imbued with order and purpose. The Roman Catholic Church provides not only spiritual insights but also a logical framework that embraces and enhances these discoveries, bridging faith with reason. This synthesis underscores the belief that all lines of inquiry, when followed earnestly, lead back to the divine blueprint.

As we proceed to explore the specific universal structures across disciplines, it becomes evident that God's providence is a cornerstone, leading us to the ultimate truth housed within the Roman Catholic Church. In the following sections, we will unravel these universal patterns and their implications, continuing to build the case for a divinely orchestrated existence.

Historical Perspectives

To appreciate the grandeur of what we term "The Divine Blueprint," it's essential to delve into the historical perspectives that have shaped our understanding of divine architecture. The Roman Catholic Church, deeply embedded in the annals of history, has always played a pivotal role in this intellectual and spiritual journey, illuminating how every universal structure points inexorably to a divine Creator. The lineage of thought spanning centuries invites us to recognize a sacred pattern that transcends individual disciplines, drawing us toward an inevitable convergence within God's church.

Historically, the Church has been the crib of Western knowledge, nurturing not just theological thought but also the seeds of science and philosophy. From the patristic writings of Church Fathers like St. Augustine to the scholastic debates led by St. Thomas Aquinas, each era contributed to unveiling the coherence of the universe with the divine mind. St. Augustine, for instance, in "Confessions" and "City of God," revealed a cosmos ordered by a supreme intelligence, laying the philosophical foundations that would be built upon by later thinkers.

The Middle Ages heralded Aquinas, whose monumental work "Summa Theologica" sought to reconcile faith with reason. Aquinas synthesized Aristotelian philosophy with Christian doctrine, arguing that reason itself is a divine gift, meant to lead us to a fuller understanding of God. This theological framework provided the Church with a robust intellectual spine, emphasizing that divine truths are not opposed to human reason but are profoundly intertwined with it.

Aquinas's Five Ways, logical arguments for the existence of God drawn from observation and reason, resound through history as monumental contributions to theistic philosophy. These arguments exemplified how rational inquiry and divine revelation are not parallel paths but conjoined itineraries leading to the ultimate truth.

In the Renaissance and Enlightenment eras, the Church encountered evolving scientific discoveries which, rather than opposing faith, often illuminated it. Figures like Galileo and Copernicus, though embroiled in conflict with ecclesiastical authorities, operated under the tacit belief that unraveling the mysteries of the universe was tantamount to understanding divine craftsmanship. It's worth noting that many scientific endeavors were underwritten by religious institutions, driven by the belief that studying creation was a form of worship.

Moving forward to the modern era, the Vatican's establishment of the Pontifical Academy of Sciences heralded an era where the Church actively engaged in scientific discourse. It stands as a testament to the Church's enduring commitment to a holistic understanding of truth, one that includes the empirical and the spiritual. Under this umbrella, questions of cosmology, biology, and even quantum physics are explored, fostering a dialogue that reminds us of the divine intricacy embedded within the fabric of reality.

Historical perspectives also invite us to consider the Church's role in shaping social ethics and human rights, viewed through the lens of divine order and moral rectitude. The unwavering stand of the Church against various forms of injustice across different epochs mirrors the moral compass rooted in Divine blueprint, asserting that human dignity and divine will are inseparably linked.

In reflecting upon these historical stages, it's apparent that the Roman Catholic Church has perpetually been a conduit for divine wisdom, guiding humanity toward an appreciation of an ordered universe reflective of an Almighty Creator. By examining how the Church has interacted with and influenced intellectual paradigms through history, we gain insights into a divine roadmap that directs hearts and minds toward God's ecclesiastical abode.

Thus, from a historical vantage, The Divine Blueprint isn't a modern conceptualization but a continuum, a narrative thread visible in the philosophical tomes, scientific treatises, and theological discourses that span epochs. This divine narrative, intricately woven and historically affirmed, leads us with unwavering certainty to the Church founded upon Peter, the rock.

Universal Structures Across Disciplines

In the grand tapestry of existence, God's fingerprints are evident in the universal structures that permeate every discipline. From the natural world to the intricate systems of the human body, from the pristine logic of mathematics to the profound tenets of philosophy, there exists a harmonious design that defies the randomness of mere chance. This divine order resonates deeply within the Roman Catholic tradition, affirming the belief that God's wisdom and providence are at the core of all creation.

Consider for a moment the structure of the DNA molecule. This double helix, discovered by Watson and Crick, is a marvel of elegant simplicity and profound complexity. Its structure is not only a blueprint for life but also a testament to the order and precision embedded in the fabric of our existence. The sequence of nucleotides, which encode genetic information, mirrors a code written by a masterful hand. The same intricate design can be seen in the spiral of a galaxy, the pattern of a nautilus shell, or the fractal branching of trees and rivers. These patterns are not random; they speak of a universal syntax that echoes the logic and grace of their Creator.

In mathematics, we encounter another realm where these universal structures manifest. The Fibonacci sequence, the golden ratio, and the symmetry of geometric shapes present themselves not as mere human constructs but as elements fundamentally woven into the universe. Mathematicians and philosophers alike have long posited that these patterns are not inventions but discoveries of an underlying order. This order points to a reality that transcends human cognition, hinting at the divine intellect that authored these constants and principles.

Philosophically, the existence of universal structures has been a subject of contemplation for millennia. Plato, in his theory of forms, suggested that the material world is a mere shadow of a higher, more perfect reality. This aligns remarkably with the Catholic understanding of the sacramental nature of existence, where material elements serve as visible signs of an invisible grace. The universality of certain moral principles, such as the inherent dignity of human life or the pursuit of truth, justice, and love, further underscores this connection. These principles are not confined to cultural or temporal boundaries; they reflect the eternal truths inscribed by a Creator.

Scientific exploration continues to unveil the sophisticated orchestration within the natural laws governing our universe. Newton's law of universal gravitation and Einstein's theory of relativity are more than just cornerstones of modern physics. They are glimpses into the profound wisdom that upholds the cosmos. When we consider the conditions necessary for life—factors so precisely balanced that even a slight variation would render life impossible—we are compelled to recognize an intentionality behind our existence. This fine-tuning of the universe is not a product of stochastic processes but indicative of a purposeful design.

As we delve deeper into the inner workings of the human body, the transcendent craftsmanship becomes even clearer. The central nervous system, with its billions of neurons forming an intricate network, is akin to a grand symphony orchestrated with unwavering precision. This remarkable system not only allows for complex thought and emotion but also aligns with the Catholic view of the human person as a profound unity of body and soul. The Church teaches that each individual is created in the image and likeness of God, a reflection of divine life in corporeal form.

These universal structures also manifest in the liturgy and sacramental life of the Roman Catholic Church. The order and rhythm of the liturgical calendar, with its seasons and feasts, mirror the cyclical patterns found in nature. This sacred time leads the faithful through a journey that echoes the natural cycles of life, death, and rebirth. The sacraments, outward signs instituted by Christ to give grace, correspond to significant moments in the human life cycle, weaving the divine into the very fabric of human existence.

In a comparative analysis of structural concepts across disciplines, one cannot help but acknowledge the similarities that suggest a common origin. Whether examining the consistent patterns in literature, music, or visual arts, we observe that these expressions of human creativity follow principles reminiscent of the natural world. Harmony, balance, and proportion are not arbitrary; they reflect a deeper order that underpins all of creation. This alignment serves to draw humanity toward the divine, facilitating an encounter with the Creator through the beauty and coherence of the created world.

Ultimately, the pervasiveness of these universal structures serves a greater purpose. They are not mere coincidences or curiosities. Rather, they are manifestations of a divine blueprint, guiding us toward an understanding of our place in the cosmos and our relationship with the Creator. By recognizing these patterns, we are invited into a deeper contemplation of God's wisdom and love, leading us to a fuller participation in the life of the Roman Catholic Church.

The universals observed across various fields of study present compelling evidence of a unified, intelligent design. They form a celestial roadmap, pointing us toward a reality that transcends our understanding yet calls us to explore it with faith and reason. In this journey, we find that the pursuit of knowledge and truth is not at odds with our faith but is a harmonious endeavor that ultimately leads us to God.

As we continue to examine the structures that bind the universe, let us do so with a sense of wonder and reverence. These universal patterns are not mere accidents; they are signatures of a divine Artist who invites us to engage with the world in a manner that is both intellectually rigorous and spiritually enriching. Through this exploration, we draw closer to the heart of the Creator, discovering that the ultimate purpose of these universals is to lead all creation back to the source of all being: God, who is fully revealed in the Roman Catholic Church.

Chapter 2: The Liturgical Calendar of the Roman Catholic Church

The liturgical calendar of the Roman Catholic Church unveils a rhythmic tapestry of time, deeply woven with divine significance and human experience. Stretching beyond mere ritual, it's a living, breathing testament to humanity's journey toward the divine, marked by sacred seasons and profound feasts. Each moment in the Church's calendar, whether it be Advent's hopeful anticipation or Easter's triumphant joy, encapsulates a part of our collective spiritual history and invites contemplation of our place in God's grand design. The calendar is not just a sequence of dates; it reflects a cosmic order, a divine choreography that synchronizes earthly existence with heavenly grace, emphasizing that every second is infused with purpose and divine intentionality. In this divine cadence, we are reminded that the Creator's hand guides the flow of time, orienting all creation towards the ultimate celebration of unity with Him.

Key Seasons and Feasts

The liturgical calendar of the Roman Catholic Church is a rich tapestry of seasons and feasts, each intricately woven to guide the faithful through a journey of spiritual renewal and reflection. This sacred chronology isn't merely an arrangement of dates and celebrations but a divine blueprint, curating human experience in alignment with God's providence and grace. Key seasons such as Advent, Christmas, Lent, Holy Week, Easter, and Ordinary Time encapsulate the fundamental mysteries of faith, inviting believers into a cyclical rediscovery of Christ's life, death, and resurrection.

Advent, the season of expectant waiting and preparation for the nativity of Christ, marks the beginning of the liturgical year. It spans four weeks and symbolizes both a retrospective reverence for the historic arrival of Christ and an anticipatory hope for His final return. This dual focus imbues the season with an inherently eschatological dimension, prompting the faithful to prepare their hearts and minds for both the joys of Christmas and the eventual culmination of time when the Savior will come again in glory.

Christmas, often perceived through a lens of cultural celebration, holds profound theological significance. This feast commemorates the Incarnation, the miraculous moment when the Word became flesh and dwelt among us. The nativity of Christ is a pivotal event, bridging the divine and human realms, and reinforcing the Catholic Church's standing as the custodian of divine truths. Amidst the festivity, the Church beckons the faithful to recognize the profundity of God's intervention in human history through the birth of Jesus.

Following Christmas, the celebration seamlessly transitions into the season of Epiphany, which underscores the revelation of Christ to the Gentiles as represented by the Magi. This feast is a clarion call to the universality of Christ's mission, emphasizing that the salvation offered by the Messiah is not constrained by ethnic or cultural boundaries but extends to all of humanity.

Lent is a period of austerity and penance, lasting forty days and recalling the time Jesus spent fasting in the desert. It is a season characterized by prayer, fasting, and almsgiving, summoning the faithful to intense spiritual introspection and transformation. The liturgical practices associated with Lent, such as the Stations of the Cross and the sacrament of Reconciliation, are designed to foster repentance and renewal, aligning the believer's journey with Christ's own path to sacrifice.

Holy Week, the crescendo of the Lenten season, comprises a series of solemn yet poignant observances. Beginning with Palm Sunday, which commemorates Christ's triumphant entry into Jerusalem, Holy Week includes pivotal moments like Maundy Thursday, recalling the Last Supper and the institution of the Eucharist. Good Friday, a day of somber reflection on Christ's Passion and Crucifixion, stands as a stark reminder of the cost of redemption. Holy Saturday, a day of silence and mourning, culminates in the Easter Vigil, an anticipation of the victorious resurrection.

Easter is the most important feast in the liturgical calendar, celebrating Jesus' resurrection from the dead and affirming the cornerstone of Christian faith—the victory of life over death. The Easter season extends over fifty days, a prolonged celebration of the resurrection that concludes with Pentecost, marking the descent of the Holy Spirit upon the apostles and the birth of the Church. This period is not merely a commemoration but a living invitation to participate in the new life offered by the risen Christ.

Ordinary Time, often misunderstood as a filler between the high seasons, is anything but ordinary. Spanning roughly thirty-four weeks, this is a time for growth and maturation in the spiritual life. It provides an opportunity for the faithful to reflect on Jesus' teachings and miracles, and to integrate these divine lessons into their daily lives. Ordinary Time reminds the believer that growth in holiness is a continuous process, requiring patience and perseverance.

In tandem with these major seasons, numerous feasts punctuate the liturgical calendar, celebrating the saints and pivotal events in Christ's life. Feasts such as the Assumption of Mary, the Transfiguration, and the Feast of Corpus Christi deepen our understanding and appreciation of the mysteries of salvation. Saints' days honor the lives of those who have exemplified Christ-like virtues, providing models of holiness and intercessors for the Church. These observances, far from mere historical remembrances, are dynamic moments of grace, fostering a communion of saints that transcends temporal boundaries.

Each feast and season encapsulates layers of symbolism and theological richness, offering a structured yet dynamic framework for the faithful to delve deeper into the mysteries of faith. They serve as pedagogical tools, educating believers in the historical, doctrinal, and spiritual tenets of Christianity. Through participation in the liturgical calendar, the Church immerses the faithful in a rhythm of worship that is both cyclical and progressive, mirroring the sanctifying journey towards final union with God.

The consistency and regularity of the liturgical calendar foster a sense of stability and continuity, grounding the believer's spiritual life in the sacred rhythms of the Church's tradition. It creates a spiritual ecosystem where the ebb and flow of high feasts and penitent seasons mirror the natural cycles of growth, decay, and renewal observed in creation. This holistic structure underscores the Church's role as a mediator of divine grace, guiding the faithful through the seasons of life with the wisdom embedded in its sacred calendar.

The liturgical calendar is thus an embodiment of God's grand design, a divine orchestration that harmonizes human experience with the eternal truths of the Gospel. Each feast and season forms an integral part of this celestial symphony, calling the faithful to a deeper understanding and lived expression of their faith. Through this sacred chronology, the Church not only commemorates the pivotal events of salvation history but actively participates in their mystery, drawing all towards the ultimate goal of union with God.

Symbolic Significance

In the rich tapestry of the Roman Catholic tradition, the liturgical calendar is far more than a sequence of dates and observances. It is a divine symphony of symbolism, deeply embroidered with layers of meaning that transcend time and space. Symbols wield incredible power; they serve as conduits for spiritual truths and divine mysteries, guiding the faithful closer to God. To understand the symbolic significance of the liturgical calendar, one must appreciate these underlying layers that weave together scripture, tradition, and the spiritual journey of the Church.

For starters, the liturgical year mirrors the life of Christ, from Advent, signifying anticipation and preparation, to Christmas celebrating the Incarnation, through Lent's penance and reflection leading to the triumphant celebration of Easter. Each season encapsulates a facet of the Christological narrative, embedding it into the rhythm of daily life. This cyclical journey is symbolic of our lifetime spiritual pilgrimage, an ongoing process of growth, renewal, and redemption.

The very architecture of the liturgical calendar, with its alternating periods of fasting and feasting, echoes the balance between asceticism and celebration that characterizes the Catholic spiritual journey. Advent and Lent, seasons of introspection and self-denial, prepare the heart for the high points of Christmas and Easter. Through this ebb and flow, the calendar maps out a path of spiritual discipline, punctuated by divine joy, a perennial reminder of the Paschal Mystery's central role in Christian life.

Similarly, the symbol of light manifests repeatedly throughout the liturgical year. From the candles of Advent to the blazing Paschal candle at Easter, light symbolizes Christ as the "Light of the World" (John 8:12). This use of light is not just symbolic but evocative, intended to kindle a spiritual awakening within the soul, reminding us that Christ's presence dispels the darkness of sin and ignorance.

The colors associated with the liturgical seasons also carry profound symbolic weight. Purple during Advent and Lent signifies penitence and royalty; white at Christmas and Easter represents purity and joy; and green during Ordinary Time symbolizes growth and hope. Each color transforms the church environment, imbuing the faithful's worship experience with a tangible sense of sacred time and divine presence.

The feasts themselves, punctuated throughout the year, serve as spiritual milestones. Solemnities like the Assumption of Mary and the feast days of saints invoke the memory of holy lives and divine interventions. These celebrations are more than mere remembrances; they are participations in the Communion of Saints, connecting the earthly Church with the heavenly realm. To celebrate a feast day is, in essence, to step outside linear time and partake in the eternal divine liturgy.

It is important to note the synchrony between the liturgical calendar and the natural world. Many feasts and fasts align with agricultural seasons and celestial events, embedding the sacred within the cyclical rhythms of creation. For instance, the timing of Easter is linked to the vernal equinox, symbolizing resurrection and new life as nature itself awakens from winter's slumber. This connection reflects the theological understanding that all of creation is imbued with divine significance, pointing us toward the Creator.

Moreover, the concept of liturgical time itself holds symbolic significance. Unlike secular time, driven by productivity and deadlines, liturgical time is kairos—a sacred realm where divine grace intersects with human chronology. It offers a reprieve from the worldly hurry, inviting the faithful to enter into God's eternal "now." This experience of sanctified time fosters a deeper awareness of God's ongoing presence and action in history and in individual lives.

Additionally, the symbols in the liturgical calendar provide a metaphysical link between the faithful and pivotal theological truths. Take, for instance, the observance of the Feast of Corpus Christi. The Eucharistic symbolism of bread and wine as the Body and Blood of Christ is a profound theological reality, encapsulated in ritual and symbol, bringing the mystery of the Incarnation and Redemption into concrete experience.

The symbolic significance extends to the liturgical practices as well—such as processions, the use of incense, and the sign of the cross. These actions are rich in meaning and purpose. A procession is an imitation of our spiritual journey toward God; incense symbolizes prayers ascending to heaven; the sign of the cross marks the believer with Christ's redemptive sacrifice. Each practice is a miniature theology lesson, reinforcing truths of the faith through symbolic action.

The Saints, too, play a crucial role in the liturgical calendar, with their feast days inviting the faithful to emulate their holy lives. Each saint represents distinct virtues and divine graces, serving as living symbols of the varied ways God's grace manifests in human life. By venerating saints, believers find role models in their spiritual journey, embodying the diverse facets of the Christian vocation.

In summary, the liturgical calendar of the Roman Catholic Church is a sophisticated tapestry of symbolic meanings that engages the faithful in an ongoing dialogue with divine mysteries. Each symbol, color, season, and feast is meticulously designed to communicate theological truths, acting as a spiritual compass guiding believers toward deeper communion with God. This interplay of symbols makes the liturgical calendar not just a chronological tool, but a profound spiritual guide, leading the faithful ever closer to the divine heart.

Chapter 3: The Periodic Table of Elements

The periodic table, a triumph of human intellect and curiosity, is not merely a chart of chemical elements; it is a magnificent symphony that hints at an underlying divine orchestration. It is a testimony to the meticulous design embedded within the universe, a design that aligns seamlessly with the principles upheld by the Roman Catholic Church. When Dmitri Mendeleev first presented this table in the 19th century, he could scarcely have imagined its resonance with the idea of a divine creator.

At its core, the periodic table reflects foundational principles that extend far beyond chemistry. Each element, with its distinctive atomic number, symbolizes a note in the cosmic symphony, intricately arranged by a maestro. This symmetry and order aren't coincidental but intentional—a pattern of divine origin. According to Catholic doctrine, God's hand guides all creation, structuring the universe in a logically coherent and mathematically precise manner that invites contemplation and awe.

Consider the arrangement of elements. Elements follow a predictable pattern, showcasing periodicity—a concept echoing the liturgy's cycles in the Roman Catholic faith. The alignment of elements by increasing atomic number and recurring properties signifies a divine fingerprint, a cosmic parallel to liturgical cycles and sacred seasons. Such periodicity reflects the Church's vision of temporal cycles imbued with spiritual significance.

Furthermore, in observing how elements interact, we unveil a cosmic narrative that speaks of unity and diversity, a key theme in Catholic theology. Hydrogen, the simplest and most abundant element, acts as a foundational building block, much like faith itself. Moving beyond hydrogen, we find an array of elements, each contributing to a larger, harmonious design, much like the diverse members of the Church create a unified body of believers.

The cosmic arrangement of these elements is a microcosm of the universe's grand design. From the smallest atom to the vast expanse of galaxies, everything falls into place according to preordained laws. This level of order suggests more than randomness; it implies intentionality, a concept deeply in line with the teachings of the Roman Catholic Church. For those willing to look, the periodic table becomes a bridge, linking science and faith, and leading all toward a greater understanding of God's divine blueprint.

Foundational Principles

The periodic table of elements stands as one of the most profound frameworks in the realm of science, a testament to the divine order embedded in the universe. Catholic scholars, alongside scientists and philosophers, have long regarded this systematic arrangement not merely as a human achievement, but as a tangible manifestation of the Creator's grand design. In understanding the periodic table, we begin to appreciate the meticulous craftsmanship with which God has designed the building blocks of the cosmos, anchoring our faith in the convergence of divine wisdom and scientific inquiry.

The elements are not randomly scattered throughout the universe; rather, they are meticulously organized into a coherent structure, an eternal testament to an intelligent designer. This principle of order is reminiscent of the theological concept of *Logos*, the divine reason and creative order. As the elements align into groups and periods, revealing predictable patterns and intricate relationships, we perceive a harmony that points directly to a cosmic intelligence far beyond human comprehension.

Just as the Roman Catholic Church serves as a spiritual scaffold guiding believers towards salvation, the periodic table serves as a scientific scaffold elucidating the material universe's fundamental truths. Both systems are rooted in a foundation of order, rationality, and interconnectedness. The periodic table's predictive power, allowing scientists to foresee the properties of yet-to-be-discovered elements, mirrors the Church's prophetic insight into the mysteries of faith and morality.

Consider the principle of periodicity itself. This concept, which predicts the recurrence of chemical properties at regular intervals, can be seen as a reflection of the cyclical nature of liturgical seasons within the Roman Catholic Church. Each liturgical cycle invites believers into deeper spiritual truths, much like how each periodic cycle unveils deeper levels of atomic structures and their properties. Can one dismiss the divine orchestration evident in these recurring patterns? It beckons both the scientist and the theologian to recognize an intelligent design knit into the very fabric of existence.

Reflecting further on order and predictability, let's consider how elements bond to form compounds. The elements do not mix haphazardly; they follow precise rules and exhibit heirarchical affinities. The clear, consistent, and purposeful nature of chemical bonding closely mirrors the order and sanctity of the sacraments within the Catholic Church. Each sacrament serves a distinct purpose and unites the faithful with God, much like each element combines under specific conditions to create new substances that sustain life and the universe.

Additionally, the hierarchical structure in which elements are arranged echoes the hierarchy within the Church. From the least to the most reactive, from simple hydrogen to complex uranium, each element occupies a specific place with unique properties and functions, all working together to maintain cosmic stability. This scientific order is reminiscent of the ecclesiastical order where each level, from laypersons to the Pope, plays a pivotal role in sustaining the spiritual edifice of the Church.

Furthermore, the idea of elements having origins, moving, and transforming resonates deeply with the Church's notion of life's journey from creation towards fulfillment in the Divine. Atomic interactions that lead to molecular formations are microcosms of human experiences that lead to spiritual growth. Both involve cycles of breaking, forming, and reforming, ultimately designed for a greater purpose. In these processes, one perceives God's hand guiding both matter and soul towards ultimate harmony.

Moreover, the process of transmutation—the conversion of one element into another through nuclear reactions—can be likened to the transformational power of God's grace. Just as the elements can undergo profound change to become new entities, so too can individuals undergo spiritual transformations through the sacraments and divine intervention. The periodic table thus not only serves as a scientific tool but also as an allegory for the transformative journey in faith.

In essence, the periodic table, a core construct in chemistry, serves as a testament to the principles of order, rationality, and beauty within God's creation. It offers not just an empirical understanding of the physical universe but also a profound glimpse into the mind of the Creator. This structured array of elements, revealing intrinsic properties and interactions, compels us to look beyond the material and recognize the divine laws governing all existence.

Given this, it is not surprising that many eminent scientists who contributed to our understanding of the periodic table were guided by a sense of the divine. Dmitri Mendeleev, who is credited with its first comprehensive formulation, saw his work not merely as a scientific endeavor but as an exploration of the natural order instituted by God. This intertwining of faith and reason among scientists throughout history underscores the unity between scientific discovery and divine revelation.

Ultimately, the foundational principles of the periodic table act as a guidepost, pointing toward a greater reality—the omnipotent hand of God shaping the universe. As we delve deeper into its intricacies, we find that every atom and molecule bears testament to God's meticulous design and purposeful order. It is through understanding these principles that faith and reason coalesce, leading us closer to the divine mysteries that govern both the material and spiritual realms.

As we journey through this exploration, remember that the Church has always upheld that faith and reason are not adversaries but allies in the search for truth. The periodic table is a prime example of how scientific inquiry can lead to a deeper understanding of divine principles. Its structure and properties are a resounding echo of the order, rationality, and beauty inherent in God's creation, reminding us of our place within this divine framework.

So let us embrace the periodic table not only as a scientific tool but as a spiritual symbol of divine order. Through understanding the principles that govern the material world, we come to appreciate the divine intelligence that orders the entire cosmos. In this way, science becomes not just a quest for knowledge but a journey of spiritual discovery, reinforcing our faith and bringing us ever closer to the truth of God's magnificent design.

Cosmic Arrangements and Their Significance

The periodic table of elements, a meticulously ordered chart of chemical entities, is more than just a scientific tool; it is a profound testament to divine intelligence. Each element, from Hydrogen to Oganesson, has its designated place, each position revealing critical information about its properties, electron configurations, and relationships with other elements. It's a marvel that invites us to ponder the deeper organizational principles of the universe, which by its very precision and order, hints at the hand of a Creator.

You see, the elements are not randomly flung across the cosmos; they show an intelligently orchestrated system. This intricate patterning informs everything from the air we breathe to the stars that twinkle in the night sky. Breaking down the periodic table allows us to appreciate how these cosmic arrangements signify a divine logic that underpins all of reality. This beautifully aligns with the Roman Catholic perspective that God is a supreme architect, meticulously designing the fabric of existence.

The elements themselves offer clues to the sublime intelligence at work in their arrangement. Consider carbon, the backbone of organic life. It forms countless compounds, ranging from the simplest forms like methane to the most complex macromolecules. Its versatile nature suggests it was specially chosen to be the cornerstone of life. Are we to believe this is mere coincidence?

Moreover, if we delve into how these elements were discovered, it adds layers of historical and scientific significance. Dmitri Mendeleev, in creating the periodic table, left gaps for elements yet to be discovered, predicting their properties with astonishing accuracy. This foreknowledge, almost prophetic, suggests that these cosmic blueprints were etched into the very fabric of the universe, waiting to be unveiled. Isn't it a leap of faith to attribute such precision to mere chance?

The periodic table also provides a framework for understanding chemical reactions and bonding. The way elements interact, form compounds, and release energy points towards a finely tuned system, calibrated to sustain life and facilitate the dynamics of the physical world. God's fingerprints seem to be all over this intricate dance of particles. It is a narrative rich with theological implications that invite both scientists and skeptics to reconsider the origin and purpose of these cosmic arrangements.

Furthermore, the table's structure—its rows and columns known as periods and groups—reveals a deeper harmony. Periodic trends like ionization energy, electron affinity, and atomic radius manifest in predictable ways, echoing a universal consistency. This regularity speaks volumes about an underlying order, a cosmic rhythm that resonates with the theological doctrine of a purposeful creation.

In each cycle of the elements, we encounter a story of transformation. Hydrogen fuses to form helium in the hearts of stars, giving birth to heavier elements in processes that fuel the cosmos. This stellar nucleosynthesis process elegantly ties together the microcosm of atomic physics with the macrocosm of astronomical phenomena, demonstrating how cosmic arrangements bear the hallmarks of intentional design. This interconnectedness is nothing short of divine orchestration.

One might also consider the anthropic principle, which suggests that the laws of nature are finely-tuned to support life. The periodic table, as a foundational component of these laws, stands as an argument for a universe tailored to human existence. If the elemental properties were tweaked even slightly, the chemical interactions that make life possible would fail. Thus, even the skeptics among us must ponder: could such a finely-tuned system arise from randomness?

Then there's the notion of essentialism, fundamental to both science and Catholic philosophy, which holds that things have an essence—a set of characteristics that define their nature. The periodic table organizes elements based on these intrinsic properties, aligning perfectly with the idea that God imbues each element with a specific role and purpose. Intrinsically, every element fulfills its divinely assigned role within the grand tapestry of creation.

Even radioactive elements, which might seem chaotic and destructive, serve vital purposes. They provide energy, medical treatments, and even offer insight into the age of the earth through radiometric dating. Their very existence fits into an orderly schema where even apparent chaos reveals deeper harmony, point again to divine wisdom. Like the many parts of the Roman Catholic Church, each element plays its part in a grand, unified design.

In theological terms, the periodic table can be seen as a modern-day parable, illustrating the kingdom of heaven through the language of science. Just as the Roman Catholic Church teaches about the unity and diversity within the Body of Christ, the periodic table presents a unity of matter composed of diverse elements. Each element, while unique, contributes to the greater good, aligned towards a harmonious cosmic order—a reflection of the divine plan.

Thus, the periodic table does more than catalog elements; it testifies to a universe characterized by order, purpose, and meaning. It's a cosmic psalm sung in the language of chemistry, pointing towards a Creator who has meticulously designed every aspect of existence. For those of faith, this arrangement validates belief, revealing a Creator who intricately weaves the physical and metaphysical realms together with precision and love. For the philosopher and scientist, it challenges the materialistic worldview, urging a reconsideration of metaphysical realities.

Understanding the periodic table within this divine framework elevates our appreciation of both science and faith. It shows that scientific exploration and religious belief need not be in opposition; rather, they complement and illuminate each other. When viewed through the lens of faith, the meticulous order and intelligibility of the periodic table confirm the belief in a purposeful Creator—an architect whose design serves as the foundation of both the physical world and the ecclesiastical universe.

In closing, the cosmic arrangements illustrated in the periodic table reveal a tapestry woven with divine precision. More than a chart of elements, it's a map of God's grand design. Each element, each interaction, serves as a testament to the divine intelligence that guides our universe. Embrace this understanding, and you see not just an ordered list of elements, but a reflection of a God who invites us all to partake in His magnificent creation, drawing us ever closer to the fullness of truth found in His Roman Catholic Church.

Chapter 4: The Human Body's Systems

Within the awe-inspiring mechanics of the human body lies a profound testament to the Creator's ingenuity, seamlessly integrating both the spiritual and biological realms. Each system, from the circulatory to the nervous, operates with a precision that transcends mere evolutionary happenstance, suggesting an intelligent design orchestrated by a divine hand. The heart pumps life through veins and arteries, much like faith courses through the veins of the body of the Church. The intricate dance of the endocrine system parallels the liturgical rhythms that guide the faithful through the sacred seasons of the Roman Catholic calendar. These systems do not function in isolation but are interconnected, reflecting the unity and interdependence found within the body of Christ's faithful. Through understanding the complexity and harmony of our own physical makeup, we gain a glimpse into the divine artistry that calls us into full communion with God's Church, affirming both our physical existence and our spiritual destiny. Such revelations not only elevate our comprehension of biology but beckon us toward a greater existential truth, one that harmonizes science with the divine architecture laid out by God within and beyond us.

Integrated Systems

The human body is a masterful integration of numerous systems working harmoniously together, a testament to the divine design crafted by the Creator. It's essential to understand that these systems do not function in isolation. Rather, they are intricately connected in ways that reveal an intelligent, purposeful design, reflecting the ultimate architect's hand at work.

Take, for instance, the cardiovascular system. It does not merely circulate blood; it delivers essential nutrients to every nook and cranny of the body, ensuring that each cell has the resources it needs to function optimally. The heart, a central organ within this system, works tirelessly in concert with other organs like the lungs, which richly oxygenate the blood before it's sent out to nourish the body. When considered alongside the nervous system, which meticulously regulates the heartbeat and adjusts blood flow in response to different stimuli, one can't help but marvel at the sophistication and foresight embodied in such a design.

This profound interconnectedness mirrors the Church's role in human society. Just as each bodily system contributes to overall health and functionality, the Roman Catholic Church acts as a guiding force, ensuring spiritual nourishment and well-being for its followers. Through the sacraments, liturgical seasons, and rich traditions, the Church harmonizes the spiritual lives of individuals, reflecting the divine will in human structures.

The respiratory and cardiovascular systems offer another illustration of integrated functionality. The close synergy between lungs and heart demonstrates how breath and blood sustain life, symbolizing the breath of the Holy Spirit animating the body of the Church. Such connections are not haphazard but deliberate, each element serving a divine purpose, much like the sacred ordinances and traditions handed down through the millennia within the Catholic Church.

In a similar vein, the digestive and endocrine systems work in tandem to convert food into energy and regulate numerous bodily functions. The precision with which enzymes break down nutrients and hormones regulate metabolism points to a design that goes beyond random chance. It speaks of a Creator who meticulously planned every aspect, ensuring that the body functions as a unified whole. This mirrors the doctrinal teachings of the Church, which serve to nourish and regulate the spiritual lives of its adherents.

We must also consider the skeletal and muscular systems, the very framework that allows for movement and support. The bones provide structure, while the muscles give the body its ability to move and act in the world. Within the context of the Church, these systems can be seen as the principles and doctrines that give it form and the laity's actions and works, which animate and bring those principles to life. Just as bones and muscles are interdependent for effective function, the Church's teachings and the actions of its members are inseparable, each relying on the other to fulfill divine purpose.

The nervous system, encompassing the brain and its vast network of nerve cells, is perhaps the most complex example of integrated systems. It orchestrates every movement, thought, and sensory experience, uniting various bodily systems into a cohesive whole. Imagine the Church as the brain, guiding and directing its followers to live purposeful lives. The nervous system's intricate design reflects a higher wisdom, a clear indicator of an intelligent Creator, paralleling the role of divine guidance in the lives of the faithful.

It's also noteworthy to mention the immune system, the body's defense mechanism against disease and infection. This system operates seamlessly with others to maintain health, exemplifying the divine notion of protection and guardianship. In the same way, the Church through its spiritual teachings and community support acts as a protective shield for the souls within its fold, warding off spiritual afflictions and offering sanctuary.

Consider also the sensory systems, which allow us to experience and interact with the environment. These systems are not just about survival; they enrich our lives, imbuing them with meaning and purpose. The experience of sight, sound, taste, touch, and smell connects us to the world around us in profound ways that elevate our existence beyond mere subsistence. Similarly, the sacraments and liturgies of the Church offer sensorial experiences that elevate our soul and connect us to the divine, enhancing both our spiritual and physical lives.

Such examples of interdependence and coordination among the body's systems compel us to recognize a higher order, a divinely instituted blueprint that mirrors the Church's role in human life. The interconnectedness seen in the human body is not an accident but a manifestation of divine wisdom. It reflects the Church's unified doctrine, emphasizing how faith and reason are not at odds but rather complementary aspects of understanding our purpose within God's grand design.

When contemplating these integrated systems, one can't help but see the parallels to the ecclesiastical order of the Roman Catholic Church—its hierarchy, its sacraments, and its communal activities. Just as the human body achieves optimal function through the harmonious interplay of its systems, the Church serves humanity best when all its parts work together in pursuit of divine will. This dynamic interplay signifies an intentional design, urging us to acknowledge and revere the ultimate Designer.

In acknowledging these wondrously integrated systems within our very being, we are led inevitably to a deeper understanding of our place within the divine order. This understanding transcends the mere biological and ventures into the spiritual, urging one to recognize the hand of God not just in the intricate workings of the human body but also in the very fabric of the universe. The Roman Catholic Church stands as the steward of this divine wisdom, guiding us towards a fuller comprehension and appreciation of the Creator's grand design.

Ultimately, the integrated systems within the human body serve as an emblem of the omnipotent Creator's wisdom, mirroring the seamless unity and purpose found within the Roman Catholic Church. In contemplating these marvels, we are drawn closer to the Divine, inspired to live our lives in consonance with the sacred blueprint laid out before us. The harmonious interplay of these systems serves as a call to recognize and embrace the profound interconnectedness that defines both our physical existence and our spiritual journey within God's Church.

Spiritual and Biological Interconnectedness

The intricate systems that make up the human body provide more than just a mechanical representation of biological processes; they serve as a profound embodiment of spiritual interconnectedness designed by our Creator. Indeed, when we delve into the marvel that is the human body, we're not merely studying a series of physiological mechanisms but rather a complex, harmonious entity reflecting divine wisdom. The Roman Catholic tradition offers deep insights into this interconnectedness, spotlighting the bond between our spiritual existence and biological form.

Understanding the human body as a finely tuned system runs parallel to appreciating the divine orchestration of the universe. Each part, whether it's the circulatory system, the nervous system, or the muscular system, works in concert with the others, displaying a unity and synchronicity that transcends mere chance. This harmony mirrors the Roman Catholic Church's teaching on the interconnectedness of the soul and body. The Catechism of the Catholic Church reminds us that "the unity of soul and body is so profound that one has to consider the soul to be the 'form' of the body" (CCC 365). It is within this unity that we find the key to understanding our true nature.

The cardiovascular system, for example, does more than just pump blood. It symbolizes the continuous and life-sustaining flow that can be likened to the spiritual nourishment provided by the Holy Eucharist. Just as the heart sends nutrient-rich blood to sustain every cell, the grace of the sacraments pumps spiritual vitality into every facet of our being. Through the celebration of the Mass and the reception of the sacraments, Catholics participate in a cycle of renewal and sustenance, reflecting the physical processes occurring within our own bodies. This mirroring further underlines the divinely instituted interconnectedness of the spiritual and the biological.

Moreover, the nervous system bridges our physical and mental capacities, serving as a conduit for the soul to interact with the physical world. This network of neurons and synapses provides an example of how the immaterial soul can exert influence over the corporeal body, illustrating a profound unity that defies simple mechanistic explanations. When we respond with compassion or act out of love, it's not just neurochemicals at work; it's the spiritual influencing the material, showcasing a seamless interdependence forged by divine design.

In terms of immune response, the way our bodies combat infections highlights an intrinsic wisdom that aligns with spiritual resilience and the fight against sin. Just as white blood cells recognize and combat foreign pathogens, so too does the human spirit, guided by the teachings of the Church, recognize and resist moral threats. This correlation between biological defenses and spiritual fortification illustrates a holistic view of human existence, one that is supported and enriched by Roman Catholic teachings.

Similarly, the human body's reproductive system is a powerful testament to the sacred interconnectedness of life. Beyond its biological purpose, it carries profound spiritual significance. The Church teaches that the procreative act is a participation in God's creative work. The coming together of a sperm and an egg to form a new life is not merely a biological event; it is a sacred moment where the physical meets the spiritual, underlined by the mystery of God's divine will. Each new life is not only a continuation of genetic material but also a testament to the soul's unique creation by God.

The skeletal system provides the framework, giving structure and support, much like the moral and ethical teachings of the Church provide a guiding framework for a life of virtue. The bones uphold the body, allowing movement and stability, just as the Church's doctrines and sacraments provide spiritual stability and direction. Our physical skeleton and our spiritual moral teachings must be strong and healthy to support a life that navigates the challenges and changes of the world with grace and purpose.

When we turn to the digestive system, its role in breaking down food and converting it into energy serves as an excellent metaphor for how spiritual reflection and Eucharistic nourishment provide us with the energy to live out our Christian vocation. Just as our digestive system absorbs nutrients necessary for our physical existence, our spiritual life requires the intake of the grace and wisdom found in the sacraments and the teachings of the Church. This process of spiritual nourishment and transformation is central to the Catholic faith and reflects the seamless integration of our biological and spiritual lives.

Even our sensory systems offer compelling parallels to spiritual truths. The capacity to see, hear, touch, taste, and smell not only enables us to interact with the world but also to experience the divine in very tangible ways. For instance, the sense of sight allows us to appreciate the beauty of creation, leading us to contemplate the Creator. The Church Fathers often speak of how physical beauty points to divine beauty, suggesting that by engaging our senses through creation, we are drawn closer to the Creator. This interplay between sensory experience and spiritual insight reinforces the interconnectedness of our spiritual and biological makeup.

Finally, let's consider the brain, the command center of our bodies, which coordinates every action, thought, and emotion. The Church teaches that our intellect and will are spiritual faculties, yet they operate through the brain. This makes the brain a crucial intermediary between the spiritual and the physical, a boundary where the two realms meet and influence each other. The Church's emphasis on the transformative power of the Holy Spirit finds a parallel in the brain's capacity for neuroplasticity—its ability to change and adapt. Just as we can train our minds to think and act righteously, influenced by the Holy Spirit, so too can our brains physically adapt through continuous learning and virtuous living.

All these reflections highlight the profound truth that our biological systems are not isolated entities but are deeply interconnected with our spiritual lives. This interconnectedness demonstrates the wisdom of our Creator, who designed the human body not only to function in a biological sense but also to reflect and fulfill spiritual realities. Roman Catholic doctrine provides a wealth of resources to help illuminate this profound unity, showing how each system within us is a testament to God's infinite wisdom and love.

In conclusion, there can be no doubt that the spiritual and biological interconnectedness of the human body is a compelling witness to the intelligent and divine design with which we are made. Each biological function echoes a spiritual truth, affirming the teachings of the Roman Catholic Church. It invites us to see ourselves not merely as physical beings but as wonderfully integrated creations of God, in whom both the spiritual and biological realms are deeply united. This sacred interconnectedness calls us to a greater awareness and reverence for our bodies as temples of the Holy Spirit and vessels of divine wisdom, ultimately leading us closer to the path that God has laid out within the embrace of His Holy Church.

Chapter 5: The Elements of the Universe

The universe is an intricate tapestry woven with threads of both mystery and revelation. To truly appreciate its majesty, one must first grasp the basic building blocks—elements that compose the vast cosmos. Think of these elements as the palette from which the Creator painted the heavens and the earth.

Modern science identifies four fundamental forces as the pillars on which all physical phenomena rest: gravity, electromagnetism, weak nuclear force, and strong nuclear force. These forces are not random, chaotic events; rather, they exhibit a coherence and order that speaks to a grander design. Without strong nuclear force, stars would not shine, and without gravity, galaxies would not bind. Each force serves a purpose, reflecting a divine intention behind their existence.

Perhaps more compelling than the forces themselves are their theological implications. The harmony and balance found in cosmological laws mirror the idea of a Creator who values order and symmetry. This isn't just food for thought; it's a banquet for the soul. Scientists often marvel at the universe's elegance, but it is within the theological lens that one truly finds purpose and design.

Consider the fine-tuning argument: the notion that specific conditions in the universe, such as the cosmological constant, are so precise that even slight deviations would render life impossible. This precision suggests not randomness, but careful calibration. It is a whisper of divine craftsmanship, an echo of a Creator's meticulous intent.

In this cosmic dance, humanity finds itself not as a mere spectator but as a participant with a unique role. The elements of the universe do more than sustain life; they beckon us to ponder the profound interconnectedness between the material and the divine. This realm of thought encourages us to not only look outward at the stars but also inward, toward our spiritual foundations.

The Roman Catholic Church, with its rich tradition and theological insights, provides a framework to understand these cosmic wonders in the light of faith. By engaging deeply with the elements of the universe, both in a scientific and theological manner, we uncover a profound truth: that all things, great and small, are interconnected by the hand of God, guiding us to His ultimate revelation through the Church.

Fundamental Forces

The universe, in its staggering immensity, is governed by a few fundamental forces that shape everything from the smallest particle to the largest galaxy. These forces are not just accidental occurrences; they reflect a divine orchestration that invites us to ponder the existence and majestic plans of our Creator. Four primary forces rule the cosmos: gravity, electromagnetism, and the strong and weak nuclear forces. Each holds unique characteristics and plays a pivotal role in the grand design of God's creation.

Gravity, often deemed the most intuitive of the fundamental forces, is responsible for the motion of planets and stars and the very structure of the cosmos. One cannot gaze upon the night sky without recognizing the delicate interplay of celestial bodies governed by this force. Gravity ensures that stars form, planets orbit, and galaxies hold their majestic spirals. This force doesn't merely attract; it unifies. It exemplifies the Church's unifying role, drawing us towards the divine center, much like how gravity pulls matter towards the core of celestial bodies.

While gravity might be easily observed, electromagnetism permeates every aspect of our daily existence, albeit often unnoticed. From light enabling us to see the world to the very electricity powering our homes, electromagnetism is a testament to the intricate design woven into the fabric of the cosmos. This force, spanning across vast distances, connects particles and waves, reinforcing the Catholic understanding of interconnectedness and communion. The unassuming electron's dance around the nucleus echoes the faithful's relationship with the Church, drawn and held in the divine orbit.

The strong nuclear force, though working at unimaginably small scales, is vital in holding the nuclei of atoms together. Without this compelling force, the universe as we know it would dissolve into chaos. It is a force of incredible strength, binding protons and neutrons tightly within the atomic nucleus. This echoes the strong bonds of faith and tradition that hold the Roman Catholic Church together, ensuring its resilience through the ages. The unwavering strength of this force serves as a reminder of the steadfastness of divine love and the immutable truths taught by the Church.

Contrastingly, the weak nuclear force, though less binding than its strong counterpart, plays a critical role in processes like radioactive decay and stellar fusion. It's this force that enables stars to burn and produce the elements necessary for life, highlighting a delicate balance designed by a meticulous Creator. The weak nuclear force demonstrates how small changes over time, subtly guided by a masterful hand, can lead to profound transformations. This mirrors the transformative power of grace and faith in the believer's soul, often working quietly yet profoundly.

Each of these forces operates within an ordered framework, a celestial dance choreographed by an omnipotent Designer. This divine orchestration echoes St. Augustine's assertion that "nature, as it were, is God's great book." Just as the pages of a book reveal a story, the forces reveal a deliberate cosmic narrative that points back to the Creator. Scientists, philosophers, and theologians alike marvel at the fine-tuning apparent in these forces, for any slight alteration would render the universe inhospitable to life. This precise calibration invites us to acknowledge and revere the intelligent design behind creation.

Throughout history, mankind has sought to understand these forces, recognizing their profound implications. In doing so, we find that faith and reason do not stand in opposition but rather complement each other. The Roman Catholic Church has long upheld this harmony, advocating for the pursuit of scientific understanding to deepen our appreciation of God's creation. The knowledge of fundamental forces doesn't diminish the divine; it amplifies our awe and reverence, affirming that faith and inquiry coexist seamlessly within the heart of the Church.

Considering these forces within the context of theological implications opens avenues for profound reflection. For instance, gravity's ubiquitous pull can be seen as a metaphor for God's omnipresence and the drawing of souls towards His grace. Electromagnetism's reach, underlying communication and light, mirrors evangelization—spreading the divine light of the Gospel across the world. The strong nuclear force's unyielding grip reflects the sacraments' strength in binding the faithful, while the weak force's subtle influence underscores the gentle yet transformative touch of God's grace in daily life.

These metaphysical reflections are not mere abstractions; they point towards the coherent integration of science and faith advocated by the Church. By understanding fundamental forces, we get a glimpse—albeit a limited one—of the Divine Architect's grand blueprint. It's a call to recognize that the Creator's hand is evident not just in the miraculous, but also in the profound principles that govern the universe. This recognition should inspire a deeper commitment to faith, encouraging believers to see the sacred in the seemingly mundane.

Moreover, the intricate dance of these forces serves as an emblem of the harmonious design underlying the cosmos. It reflects a universe that is not random, but purposeful, designed to sustain life and reflect divine glory. As we delve into scientific exploration, we unearth the layers of an awe-inspiring creation that continually points back to its Creator. The Roman Catholic Church, through its tradition and teachings, invites us to see these revelations not as mere scientific phenomena but as sacred insights into the mind of God.

In conclusion, recognizing the fundamental forces reveals the tangible aspects of God's intelligent design. As gravity, electromagnetism, and the strong and weak nuclear forces weave the cosmos together, they point to a higher purpose and meticulous craftsmanship. These forces invite us to deepen our understanding and appreciation of creation's complexity, reinforcing the Catholic view that all truth—scientific and spiritual—leads back to the Divine. In contemplating these forces, we are drawn closer to the grandeur of God's eternal Church, echoing the harmonious interplay of faith and reason in our continuous quest for truth.

Theological Implications in Cosmology

Cosmology, traditionally the domain of astronomers and physicists, takes on a profound depth when examined through a theological lens. For centuries, the vast expanse of the cosmos has been a source of awe and wonder, raising questions that traverse both the material and the spiritual realms. To begin comprehending the theological implications of cosmology is to undertake a journey that requires no small measure of intellectual curiosity and faith.

At the heart of this intersection lies a fundamental question: What does the structure and nature of the universe tell us about the existence and nature of God? Roman Catholic theology posits that the universe, in all its complexity and order, reflects a divine blueprint—the handiwork of an omnipotent creator. This principle is deeply rooted in scripture and tradition, linking the patterns and phenomena of the physical universe with divine will and purpose. The cosmos itself, with its grandiose scale and intricate laws, can be seen as a manifestation of God's grandeur and meticulous design.

The Book of Genesis offers a powerful narrative regarding the creation of the universe, one that Roman

Catholics interpret as an affirmation of God's omnipotence and omniscience. In this light, cosmology is not just a scientific endeavor but a theological affirmation that every star, planet, and cosmic law was intentionally crafted by a higher power. This belief enriches our understanding of cosmology, suggesting that the cosmic order is an extension of divine wisdom, guiding us towards greater spiritual truths.

Moreover, the concept of the 'Fine-Tuned Universe' presents a compelling argument for the existence of a divine creator. Scientists have noted that the fundamental constants of nature appear to be precisely calibrated to allow for the existence of life. Were these constants to vary even slightly, the universe as we know it could not sustain life. For many theologians and philosophers, this fine-tuning is not a mere coincidence but evidence of a purposeful, intelligent designer—God. It suggests that the universe was created with intention and foresight, aligning with the Roman Catholic view that God's providence is found in all aspects of creation.

Another theological dimension in cosmology is the notion of eschatology—or the study of the end times. Catholic eschatology often includes a cosmic dimension, anticipating a new heaven and new earth as part of the promised fulfillment of God's kingdom. This perspective provides not only hope but also a sense of purpose to the unfolding story of the cosmos, affirming that the material universe is intrinsically connected to God's ultimate plan for salvation and eternal life.

The expansion of the universe and the Big Bang theory also hold significant implications. The Big Bang—considered by many as the initial 'moment' of creation—can be interpreted theologically as the divine fiat, echoing the biblical "Let there be light." Such interpretations enrich the dialogue between faith and science. They suggest that cosmological discoveries do not undermine theological beliefs but rather illuminate the grandeur and mystery of God's creating act. They reinforce the position that science and faith are not in opposition but are complementary ways of understanding the same reality.

In this context, the Roman Catholic Church has often embraced scientific advancements, viewing them as a path to deeper theological insights. The Vatican Observatory, one of the oldest astronomical research institutions in the world, symbolizes the Church's commitment to this harmonious relationship. Its mission has always been to show that faith and reason, spirituality and science, are not adversaries but allies in the quest for truth. This guiding principle supports the belief that by exploring the cosmos, we are simultaneously uncovering the layers of divine creation.

Pope Pius XII famously endorsed the Big Bang theory as compatible with the Catholic doctrine of Creation, noting that such scientific insights bring us closer to understanding the "Fiat Lux" moment. Each telescopic discovery, each mathematical equation modeling the universe, each theoretical breakthrough, can be viewed as a divine invitation to delve deeper into the mysteries of faith. This perspective encourages believers to see scientific pursuit as a form of divine worship, an acknowledgment of God's infinite wisdom and creativity.

Let's not forget the moral and ethical implications of cosmological findings. The vastness of the universe places humanity in a humbling context, reminding us of our stewardship role as outlined in Genesis. Feeling small beneath the starry heavens doesn't diminish our importance but highlights our responsibility to care for creation. It aligns with the Catholic teaching of the imago Dei, the belief that we are created in the image of God, entrusted with the guardianship of our world and the universe we inhabit.

Finally, this exploration prompts philosophical reflections on existential questions such as the meaning of life, our place in the universe, and our relationship with the divine. It challenges skeptics and believers alike to ponder the origins of everything we see and know. The intricate order of the cosmos invites us to consider whether such harmony could arise from chaos or whether it is the work of an intelligent designer.

In conclusion, the theological implications in cosmology provide a rich tapestry that not only affirms the divine craftsmanship of the universe but also strengthens the resonance between faith and reason. Through the lens of cosmology, we witness a universe that echoes the glory of God, offers a testament to divine order, and calls us to a deeper understanding of our purpose within this vast and splendid creation. Such reflections do not merely satisfy intellectual curiosity; they elevate our spirits, reaffirming the central tenet of Roman Catholicism—that the universe is a magnificent testament to God's eternal wisdom and love, guiding us all towards His divine Church.

Chapter 6: Mathematical Universals

Mathematics, often described as the language of the universe, offers an almost mystical connection to the divine. Its principles seem intrinsic, existent beyond the bounds of human creation or discovery. At its core lie theorems and proofs echoing an underlying, divine symmetry. Let's delve into this sacred geometry that binds the cosmos.

Consider the principle of *pi*. This irrational number, forever captivating in its unending, non-repeating sequence, serves as a cornerstone in various branches of mathematics. From the simple circle to the complexities of quantum physics, pi is ubiquitous. Its presence impels us to ponder: Could such an elegant constant have emerged from chaos, or does it point to a grand Designer?

Equally compelling is the Fibonacci sequence, another numerical marvel intertwining nature and mathematics. From the arrangement of leaves on a stem to the spirals of galaxies, Fibonacci numbers manifest themselves in seemingly improbable places. Is it mere coincidence, or is it a sign of divine craftsmanship, guiding the universe with delicate precision?

Prime numbers, the 'atoms' of the mathematical world, further underscore a sense of ordained structure. Foundational yet enigmatic, primes have fascinated mathematicians for centuries. They appear irregular, scattered without apparent order, yet they are the building blocks for countless theorems. This apparent randomness, so finely tuned, reveals what Saint Augustine termed "numbers written by the fingers of God."

Many renowned mathematicians and philosophers have articulated the intrinsic beauty of mathematical laws. The intricate web of equations and relationships uncovered by human inquiry suggests not accidental emergence but rather a preordained harmony. Such reflections draw us closer to the idea that mathematics is not just a tool but a glimpse into the mind of the Creator.

Mathematical structures, from simple arithmetic to complex calculus, illustrate a universe governed by order, not anarchy. This order bespeaks a higher intelligence, a divine Mind that not only created these patterns but imbued them with purpose. These universals guide us, whispering the existence of a supreme Architect whose blueprint for reality aligns with the sacred doctrines of the Roman Catholic Church.

Core Theorems and Proofs

In the mathematical world, certain theorems and proofs stand as pinnacles of human understanding— testimonies to the harmony and order of creation. These core theorems are not mere abstract concepts; they are manifestations of Divine intellect, demonstrating a higher order, purpose, and design inherent in the universe. Through them, we see glimpses of the Creator's signature in the language of mathematics, which serves as the universal language of creation.

One of the most profound examples of this divine symmetry is the Pythagorean Theorem. Attributed to Pythagoras, this fundamental principle in geometry states that in a right-angled triangle, the square of the hypotenuse is equal to the sum of the squares of the other two sides. This theorem not only serves as a cornerstone in Euclidean geometry but also illustrates the inherent order within the cosmos. The relationship it describes is almost too perfect, suggesting a design so intricate that chance becomes an implausible explanation.

The proof of the Pythagorean Theorem, occurring in myriad forms across cultures and epochs, underlines the universality of this mathematical truth. Whether through algebraic manipulation, geometric dissection, or logical reasoning, the consistent result points to a singular, coherent structure underpinning reality. This coherence is indicative of a divine intellect, orchestrating a world of precision and predictability. The omnipotence of God, as perceived through the lens of the Roman Catholic faith, echoes in the unwavering truth of such theorems.

Another cardinal theorem is Fermat's Last Theorem, which posits that there are no whole number solutions for the equation $a^n + b^n = c^n$ for n greater than 2. This theorem remained an enigmatic puzzle for over three centuries, challenging the finest minds until Andrew Wiles provided a proof in 1994. The proof required advanced concepts from algebraic geometry and modular forms—fields that themselves burgeoned from the seeds of simpler, more foundational theorems. The elegant complexity of Wiles' proof is a testament to the layered intelligence of the design embedded in mathematics.

One cannot ignore Gödel's Incompleteness Theorems when discussing core mathematical proofs. Kurt Gödel's groundbreaking work in the 20th century shook the foundations of mathematical thought, revealing that any sufficiently powerful formal system cannot be both complete and consistent. This means there will always be true statements within the system that it cannot prove. Gödel's theorems hint at the limitations of human understanding and the infinite depth of divine knowledge. They serve as a humbling reminder of the transcendence of the Creator's intellect, eternally beyond the grasp of finite human reasoning.

Consider also the Euler's Identity, often hailed as the most beautiful theorem in mathematics. It links five of the most important constants in mathematics: e, i, π, 1, and 0, in the elegant formula $e^{(i\pi)} + 1 = 0$. This identity is mesmerizing in its simplicity and profundity, uniting concepts from algebra, calculus, and complex analysis in a single, elegant equation. For many, Euler's Identity is more than just a mathematical curiosity; it suggests a deeper, almost mystical order in the universe, hinting at the unified nature of divine laws.

The universality of these theorems across cultures and historical periods also suggests an archetypal structure, a blueprint of divine origin that transcends human invention. Mathematics, far from being a human construct, is a discovery of the framework within which

God's creation operates. This perspective aligns with the Roman Catholic understanding of God as the ultimate law-giver, whose wisdom permeates every aspect of creation, from the cosmological to the microscopic.

To elaborate further on this divine order, we must turn to the theory of prime numbers and the Riemann Hypothesis. Prime numbers are the building blocks of mathematics; every whole number is either a prime or a product of primes. The distribution of prime numbers appears random, yet the Riemann Hypothesis, a conjecture dating from the 19th century, suggests an underlying pattern governed by the zeros of the Riemann zeta function. Though unproven, this hypothesis captivates mathematicians because it holds the potential to unlock deeper realms of mathematical and, consequently, cosmic order. The hidden regularity among primes whispers of an elegant divine design waiting to be unraveled.

Mathematical proofs, by their nature, require rigorous logical structures, showcasing the inherent rationality that God imbued in creation. The act of proving a theorem is almost a sacred ritual, an intellectual pilgrimage that brings us closer to understanding the divine order. When a mathematician gazes upon a completed proof, they are witnessing a fragment of the eternal, a piece of God's blueprint revealed.

Beyond individual theorems, overarching mathematical structures like group theory and topology further demonstrate the elegance of divine design. Group theory, for instance, explores the algebraic structures known as groups, which encapsulate symmetry. Symmetries are visible in everything from crystal structures to the orbits of planets, indicating a unifying principle—one that reflects the ordered beauty of God's creation.

Topology, the study of properties that remain invariant under continuous deformations, delves into spaces and dimensions, revealing hidden connectivity and continuity. It's as if the universe is a finely woven tapestry, each thread linking to another in intricate patterns, making a whole that is unfathomably greater than the sum of its parts. These are not arbitrary or human-imposed concepts; they are discernments of the divine threadwork that sustains reality.

Moreover, the universality of mathematical truths transcends temporal and cultural boundaries. The number pi (π), for example, is the same constant in the circles of ancient Babylonia, the geometry of Euclid, and the calculations of contemporary physicists. This constancy reflects a meta-universal truth, suggesting that mathematics is not created but discovered. As such, its ultimate discoverer is God, the eternal geometer, whose work we endeavour to decode.

In conclusion, the core theorems and proofs in mathematics are more than just intellectual achievements; they are encounters with the divine. Through them, one glimpses the flawless logic and ordered beauty of God's creation. Each theorem, each proof, is a stepping stone toward greater understanding—a signpost pointing to the transcendent intellect of the Creator. The Roman Catholic faith posits that God is the author of all truth, including mathematical truths, and these core theorems and proofs are but a fraction of His infinite wisdom. Thus, as we unravel these mathematical universals, we not only solve intellectual puzzles but also partake in a sacred journey, a pilgrimage towards the ultimate truth, leading us into the embrace of God's Church.

Divine Order in Mathematics

Mathematics is often heralded as the language of the universe, a language through which God's grand design can be discerned. The concept of divine order in mathematics invites us to gaze into the symmetrical precision and coherence that underpin the fabric of our reality. When one examines mathematical universals—adequately titled given their applicability across various sciences and philosophies—one cannot help but sense a deeper, almost sacred pattern. This divine mathematical tapestry reveals itself not just in theorems and proofs but resonates through the very essence of existence.

Consider the Fibonacci sequence, a series of numbers that shows startling regularity in nature. This sequence appears in everything from the spirals of galaxies to the arrangement of leaves on a stem. For many Roman Catholics and those inclined towards theological reflection, these patterns are not mere coincidence. They echo the mindful intention of a divine creator, a God who embeds His fingerprint in the very algorithms that describe the natural world. The sequence manifests a beautiful interplay between numbers and nature, bridging the gap between abstract thought and tangible phenomena.

Skeptics may argue that these patterns arise out of natural selection or other purely scientific explanations. While these perspectives offer valuable insights, they often fall short in addressing the deeper 'why' questions. Why does nature prefer such mathematical harmony? Why should there be an aesthetic loveliness in the numerical structures underlying everything from atomic interactions to cosmic phenomena? The divine order in mathematics doesn't just point to an intelligent designer; it amplifies the theological message that God imbues His creation with purpose and meaning.

Another quintessential example is the Golden Ratio, often denoted by the Greek letter phi (ϕ). This ratio, approximately 1.618, frequently appears in art, architecture, and even the human body. It offers a compelling glimpse into the divine precision in God's creation. Phi's occurrence in the nautilus shell, the Parthenon, and Leonardo da Vinci's "Vitruvian Man" speaks to a universal aesthetic codified into the very structure of existence. Such recurring motifs in both man-made and natural works are more than mathematical marvels; they reflect a divine symmetry, aligning humanity's creativity with God's own design principles.

The Pythagorean theorem is yet another example that illuminates divine order. This simple yet profound relation between the sides of a right triangle reveals fundamental truths about spatial relationships. The theorem's elegance and universal applicability stand as a testament to a deeper, inherent order crafted by a divine hand. Its utility spans architectural design, navigation, and even the fundamentals of quantum physics. Seen through the lens of faith, the Pythagorean theorem does not merely describe geometrical relationships; it serves as a divine signpost, guiding us to the realization that all creation is meticulously orchestrated by an ultimate geometer—God Himself.

Furthermore, mathematical constants like Pi (π) and Euler's number (e) demonstrate an omnipresent consistency in our universe. Pi, representing the ratio of a circle's circumference to its diameter, is an irrational number that appears in various equations describing waves, circles, and even the behavior of the universe at large. Euler's number, pivotal in natural logarithms, compound interest calculations, and complex number analysis, similarly underscores a divine consistency.

These constants serve as crucial cornerstones in higher mathematics, suggestive of a consistent, ordered reality that is comprehensible and discoverable because it was designed by an omniscient and omnipotent Creator.

In the realm of number theory, prime numbers stand out as another miraculous feature of mathematics. These 'building blocks' of numbers have fascinated mathematicians for centuries. Primes appear somewhat randomly within the overall system of integers, yet they are essential for various cryptographic algorithms and thereby, indispensable in our digital age. The unpredictable yet foundational nature of prime numbers suggests a divine mathematical puzzle, one that intrigues and challenges humanity to reach deeper levels of understanding. Could it be that God introduces such complexities to invite us into a lifelong exploration of His infinite wisdom?

Infinity itself, a concept both awe-inspiring and baffling, further emphasizes the divine aspect of mathematics. Whether we consider the infinitesimal scale of calculus or the expansive reach of cosmic distances, infinity beckons us to acknowledge our limitations while inviting us to ponder God's boundlessness. In Cantor's work on different sizes of infinity, we glimpse a deeper theological parallel: just as there are infinite sets larger than others, so too is God's infinity beyond our finite comprehension. This beckons us to humility and reverence, recognizing our small yet significant place in His grand design.

Moreover, symmetry and fractals present a beautiful paradox: chaotic complexity and order coexist. Fractals, like the Mandelbrot set, reveal an infinite self-similarity, where zooming in perpetually reveals finer intricate details mirroring the whole. Such a phenomenon reminds us of God's omnipresence—simultaneously grand and intimately detailed. This mirrors the Catholic understanding of the Immanent and Transcendent God: omnipotent over vast expanses, yet intricately aware of every minute detail.

Intriguingly, even the pursuit of mathematical proofs and solutions embodies a form of divine quest. The search for solutions to longstanding problems like Fermat's Last Theorem or the Riemann Hypothesis can be seen as a pilgrimage, a journey towards greater truth and comprehension. Each theorem proved, each problem solved, is a testament to the harmony between human inquiry and divine revelation. Just as saints sought to unravel the mysteries of divine love and grace, mathematicians endeavor to uncover the mysteries embedded in the language of numbers. This journey of discovery is itself a reflection of the divine order, inviting humanity to continually seek, question, and ultimately marvel at the intricacy of God's creation.

When these various mathematical elements are viewed collectively, they do more than highlight individual instances of divine order; they form a cohesive narrative underscoring God's omnipotent design. They invite us to peer beyond the veil of mere physical phenomena into a realm of spiritual reflection, where each formula and number narrates a story of divine splendor and intentionality. This alignment between mathematical purity and divine creativity not only amplifies faith but also intellectually enriches our understanding of God's universe

In sum, mathematics isn't just an abstract human construct; it is a bridge between the finite and the infinite, a testament to a universe imbued with divine order and purpose. For the readers, encompassing Roman Catholics, scientists, and philosophers alike, this exploration reveals that the elegance and complexity of mathematical universals point beyond themselves. They illuminate the grandeur and meticulousness of a Creator who woven these truths into the very fabric of existence, urging all towards a deeper contemplation of His infinite wisdom and ultimately guiding them into the fold of His Holy Church.

Chapter 7: Scientific Theorems and Laws

The elegance of scientific theorems and laws reflects the divine order permeating our universe, acting as a testament to God's meticulous creation. Whether we examine Newton's laws of motion or the intricacies of quantum mechanics, we find patterns so precise and consistent that they invariably point to a higher intelligence. The Roman Catholic Church, which has long been a patron of scientific inquiry, recognizes these laws not as arbitrary phenomena but as manifestations of God's rational design. Every formula and principle underscores the Creator's invisible hand, seamlessly integrating the natural world and compelling even the skeptics to ponder the divine origin behind these universal truths. This symphony of theorems and laws doesn't merely describe our world; it glorifies the One who designed it, hinting that all roads of knowledge and discovery ultimately lead to His Church.

Understanding Nature

To truly appreciate the laws and theorems that govern our world, it is essential to understand nature in its full splendor and complexity. Nature is the grand tapestry through which we interpret the interplay of various scientific principles. When we look deeply, what we find is a remarkable coherence, an underlying order that seems almost miraculous. This coherence is not random or incidental but a reflection of divine intentionality, a glimpse into the mind of the Creator.

Consider the elegance of the natural laws that govern our universe—from Newton's laws of motion to Einstein's theory of relativity. These laws offer us a consistent framework within which we can predict and understand the natural world's behavior. They are not arbitrary; rather, they reveal a level of precision that hints at a grand design. From the motion of celestial bodies to the quantum particles that make up our physical universe, each aspect operates within an ordered system, suggesting an intelligent Creator behind it all.

Understanding nature involves recognizing the intricate connections between its various components. Take, for instance, the water cycle. Rain falls from clouds, nourishes the earth, evaporates back into the atmosphere, and condenses to form clouds again. This cycle is both simple and profoundly complex, illustrating how natural systems are interconnected in ways that sustain life. So, too, are the scientific theorems and laws that describe these phenomena interconnected, pointing to a coherent design that aligns with the theological view of a purposeful Creator.

Moreover, the inherent beauty and simplicity found in natural theorems and laws often lead us to profound realizations. The Fibonacci sequence, observable in the arrangement of leaves, flowers, and even galaxies, speaks to a universal mathematical order. Such patterns are not merely coincidental; they serve as moving reminders that the universe operates under principles far grander than mere chance. Here, faith and reason converge, merging scientific understanding with a divine framework.

Intellectual history has shown us that some of the greatest scientists were also deeply spiritual people. Isaac Newton, for example, saw his work as a way to understand God's creation. He marveled at the intricate details of the natural world, viewing them as evidence of divine craftsmanship. This perspective provides a rich, multidimensional understanding of scientific inquiry, where the study of nature is also a spiritual endeavor.

Indeed, the more we delve into the complexities of the natural world, the more evident it becomes that our universe is finely tuned. Whether through the precise constants that govern physical laws or the delicate balances that allow life to flourish, these observations consistently point us back to a Creator. The anthropic principle, which posits that the universe's laws appear tailor-made for life, further supports this notion. Such precise calibrations are challenging to explain purely through random processes, suggesting instead a purposeful design.

Natural laws also demonstrate a unique blend of predictability and complexity. This duality is fascinating because it is within this space that we can participate in the joy of discovery, unveiling more of the Creator's work. Each new scientific breakthrough reveals another layer of this divine puzzle, allowing humanity to peer ever deeper into the workings of God's creation.

From a theological viewpoint, nature serves as a profound means of revelation. The concept of natural theology asserts that by studying the natural world, we can gain insights into the divine. The Book of Proverbs elucidates this idea, suggesting that one can discern much about the Creator through His creation. Every tree, every molecule, and every natural law is a testament to a deliberate, intelligent design.

The ecological systems that sustain life on Earth further exemplify this divine craftsmanship. The way ecosystems maintain balance, how species interact symbiotically, and how energy flows through these systems all reflect a deeper level of purpose and intentionality. It's as if each element in nature is a brushstroke in a grand, divine masterpiece. And in this exquisite painting, human beings are invited not merely as observers but as participants who can appreciate and steward this creation.

Modern science, when viewed through the lens of faith, doesn't diminish the sense of wonder but amplifies it. Advancements in quantum mechanics, genetic mapping, and cosmology have revealed complexities that challenge and expand our understanding. These discoveries do not negate the presence of a Designer; rather, they enhance our appreciation of the scope and scale of the Creator's work. By understanding nature better, we draw closer to understanding God's intentions.

Sometimes, understanding nature also requires us to admit our limitations. The more we learn, the more we realize how much remains unknown. This humility fosters a deeper sense of awe and reverence, urging us to recognize that the study of nature is an ever-ongoing journey. In this journey, both faith and reason serve as guides, helping us navigate the vast expanse of the Creator's universe.

Thus, the comprehension of nature does not merely remain within the confines of scientific inquiry; it evolves into a spiritual endeavor. By decoding the mysteries of the natural world, we find ourselves entranced by the magnitude of divine complexity. Every discovery becomes a piece of evidence pointing not to chaotic happenstance but to a thoughtful, omnipotent Creator whose ultimate design invites all to marvel and believe.

The Roman Catholic Church, with its rich tradition of integrating faith and reason, stands as a beacon guiding us toward this holistic understanding. Its teachings emphasize that the laws governing the natural world are a language through which God communicates his creativity and wisdom. In aligning with this perspective, we come to see every scientific law, every natural occurrence, as part of a grander, divine narrative that invites us all to deeper faith.

In conclusion, understanding nature is not a purely scientific endeavor but a spiritual voyage that affirms our place within divine creation. The laws and theorems that govern the natural world provide not only pathways for intellectual exploration but also avenues for spiritual enlightenment. Through them, we see the invisible hand of the Creator, inviting all to acknowledge, understand, and ultimately embrace the wisdom and love embedded in the magnificent tapestry of nature.

The Creator's Invisible Hand

It's easy to view scientific theorems and laws as impersonal edicts of nature, immutable rules governing the universe with mechanical precision. Yet, a discerning eye sees beyond the superficial layers of equations and constants. Many of our greatest scientists, from Isaac Newton to Albert Einstein, saw their discoveries not as ends in themselves but as manifestations of a higher order. They perceived the subtle yet unmistakable guidance of a Creator, whose invisible hand orchestrates every facet of existence.

Consider, for instance, Newton's law of universal gravitation. While it mathematically explains how objects attract one another, it also hints at a greater orchestration. Gravity ensures planets revolve around stars, moons around planets, creating a harmonious celestial ballet. To anyone with spiritual insight, this harmony is not the product of random forces but the deliberate choreography of a divine hand. This intricate gravitational dance maintains both order and beauty in the cosmos, aligning perfectly with the idea of a purposeful creation.

Einstein's theory of relativity further deepens this awe. His equations reveal a universe where space and time are intertwined, where matter tells space how to curve and space tells matter how to move. Einstein himself remarked that he wanted to know "how God created the world," indicating his intuition that the laws he uncovered were more than mere scientific principles; they were insights into the Creator's design. The elegance and symmetry in relativity are a testament to the divine architect who forms the underpinning of all that exists.

Take the second law of thermodynamics. It tells us that in a closed system, entropy—or disorder—tends to increase. This principle has profound cosmological and philosophical implications. At first glance, it might appear to point towards a universe winding down into chaos. However, this natural tendency towards disorder also emphasizes the extraordinary organizing power of life and consciousness. The very existence of ordered systems, right down to the cellular complexity in living beings, speaks of a guiding, creative force counterbalancing entropy. A force that aligns perfectly with the notions of a sustaining Creator who is continually active in His creation.

The fine-tuning of the universe is another striking example of the Creator's meticulous craftsmanship. Physical constants, such as the gravitational constant, the electromagnetic force, and the cosmological constant, are set at values so precise that even the slightest deviation would render the universe uninhabitable. Scientists often marvel at this "fine-tuning," acknowledging that the probability of these constants aligning by chance is infinitesimally small. For believers, this fine-tuning is no accident but a deliberate act of a Creator who designed the universe to support life, particularly human life. It is, in essence, a cosmic invitation to recognize one's place in the divine order.

The very laws of nature that scientists study with such rigor can be seen as a divine language—an encoded script in which the universe has been written. Mathematics, often described as the language of the universe, reveals patterns and symmetries that are astonishing in their elegance. The Fibonacci sequence, fractals in nature, and the golden ratio all point towards an inherent beauty and order that transcends mere numbers. They urge contemplation of their origin and purpose, leading to the realization that the Creator's hand is at work, guiding the formation of these mathematical truths.

One cannot overlook quantum mechanics and its startling revelations about the fundamental nature of reality. Quantum entanglement defies classical notions of locality and causality, suggesting that particles can be interconnected across vast distances. This phenomenon has philosophical and theological implications that are astonishing. It hints at an underlying unity and interconnectedness in the fabric of reality, resonating with the idea of a Creator who is omnipresent and immanent in His creation. Quantum mechanics challenges our understanding, pushing us to recognize the mystery and majesty of divine intervention in the minutest aspects of existence.

It's important to address the skepticism that often arises when discussing divine implications in scientific laws. Skeptics argue that invoking a Creator is an unnecessary hypothesis, a relic of a pre-scientific age. However, this viewpoint fails to appreciate the depth and nuance of the question. The Creator's invisible hand isn't seen in what science can't explain but in the very intelligibility and consistency of the natural world that science has uncovered. The coherence and reliability of natural laws make sense within the framework of a rational, ordered creation by a purposeful Creator. This alignment is not an argument from ignorance but from recognition—seeing the divine logic embedded in the very fabric of reality.

For the philosophical mind, the existence of scientific laws themselves begs the question of their origin. Why should the universe adhere to discoverable laws rather than chaotic randomness? This is the essence of the "lawgiver" argument, suggesting that the presence of consistent laws indicates a Lawgiver. In Roman Catholic theology, this Lawgiver is understood as God, whose orderly nature is reflected in the universe He designed. This theological perspective harmonizes with the scientific understanding of a universe governed by laws, suggesting a deeper purpose and intentionality behind them.

Modern discoveries in neuroscience and biology also echo the Creator's invisible hand. The complexity of the human brain, with its billions of neurons and synapses, orchestrates consciousness and thought in ways that still baffle scientists. The profound design observable in biological systems—from the intricate mechanisms of DNA to the elegant functionality of cellular processes—

demonstrates an astonishing degree of sophistication and purpose. For those who see beyond the material, these biological marvels are signposts pointing to a divine Designer whose wisdom is inscribed in every living cell.

Ultimately, the synthesis of science and faith offers a fuller, more profound understanding of the universe. The Creator's invisible hand manifests not just in the grandeur of galaxies but also in the simplicity of a falling apple, in the whisper of quantum fluctuations, and in the patterns of life itself. It invites every scientist, skeptic, philosopher, and believer to look beyond the equations and see the divine artistry at work.

In embracing this view, one recognizes the Roman Catholic Church's efforts to bridge faith and reason, highlighting the compatibility and mutual enrichment of scientific discovery and theological insight. The Church has long upheld the notion that true science and true religion cannot be in conflict, for they both seek truth. This harmony between faith and science exalts our understanding of the Creator, asserting that every law, theorem, and constant is not only a testament to the brilliance of human inquiry but also a profound revelation of the Creator's eternal hand guiding all creation towards its ultimate purpose.

Chapter 8: Philosophical Universals

As we transition from our exploration of scientific theorems and laws, we find ourselves entering a domain where abstraction takes precedence: the realm of philosophical universals. Philosophers through the ages have battled with the notion of universals, pondering the existence of concepts that stand beyond the particular instances we observe in reality. This chapter delves into the central ideas and arguments that support the existence of philosophical universals and their divine origins, adding another layer to our understanding of God's intricate design.

At its core, the philosophical problem of universals wrestles with a simple yet profound question: Do abstractions such as beauty, justice, or numbers exist independently of the human mind, or are they merely social constructs? This brings us to two primary camps in the philosophical discourse – Realism and Nominalism. Realists argue that universals exist outside and independent of human thought. They assert that there is a realm where these universals, such as the concept of "redness" shared by all red objects, exist objectively and eternally. On the other hand, nominalists contend that universals are nothing more than names or labels that humans use to group objects with similar characteristics. They maintain that only individual objects exist, not the abstract properties they share.

Throughout history, several key figures have contributed to this debate. Plato, for instance, was a staunch realist who proposed the existence of a transcendent world of Forms. According to him, every object in our sensory world is an imperfect representation of its perfect Form in the world of Ideas. For Plato, these Forms were eternal, immutable, and divine, reflecting an ideal that our worldly objects could only strive to replicate. Aristotle, while a student of Plato, introduced a more nuanced perspective. He posited that universals do exist but not in a separate realm; they are intrinsic to the objects themselves. Thus, when we say two objects share the same "redness," that quality is an integral part of each object, rather than a standalone essence.

Medieval scholars such as Thomas Aquinas built on these Greek foundations, examining the implications of universals within a theological framework. For Aquinas, the existence of universals was undeniable, and he saw them as a testament to the divine intellect. God's knowledge, he claimed, encompasses all possible universals, and these are reflected in the ordered reality we experience. Aquinas, aligning with his Aristotelian leanings, believed that universals were present both in God's mind and in the material world.

One can't discuss the existence of philosophical universals without addressing their implications. If universals such as goodness, truth, and beauty are real and intrinsic parts of the universe, then they suggest a deliberate and intelligent design. These qualities are not merely accidental byproducts of a chaotic existence but rather intentional aspects of creation. This gives weight to the argument of a divine architect, a being who not only brought the cosmos into existence but did so with a specific order and purpose in mind.

This leads us to the notion of natural law, which is rooted in the belief that moral principles are universal and can be discerned through human reason. The concept of natural law resonates deeply within Roman Catholic teachings, aiming to bridge the gap between divine wisdom and human existence. Philosophers like John Finnis and Germain Grisez have elaborated on this, arguing that human acts are good or bad depending on whether they adhere to these universal principles. If moral universals exist, they guide us towards goodness, reflecting the divine order established by God.

In light of such a discussion, one might wonder about the role of language and how it relates to these universal concepts. Ludwig Wittgenstein, a philosopher who profoundly influenced 20th-century thought, argued that the limits of our language are the limits of our world. Language, in his view, shapes and constrains our understanding of reality. Nevertheless, the persistence of universals in human communication indicates that these concepts transcend individual languages and cultures. They point to something beyond the arbitrary construction of words, reinforcing the idea of a built-in structure to human cognition – a structure that many believe is divinely ordained.

We can't ignore the role that personal experience and perception play in shaping our understanding of universals. Kant, for instance, proposed that while we might never access the noumenal world, the world as it is in itself, our minds are equipped with inherent categories that shape our perception of reality. These categories, such as space, time, and causality, are not learned but innate, suggesting an intrinsic order to human cognition reflective of a higher logic.

The argument for a divine architect gains further support when we consider the unifying power of universals across various disciplines. Whether in mathematics, ethics, or aesthetics, universal principles and patterns emerge repeatedly, hinting at a coherent and purposeful design. This coherence suggests compatibility with a theistic interpretation of the universe's origins. These philosophical universals act as threads in the vast tapestry of creation, intricately woven to reflect divine intention.

Therefore, acknowledging philosophical universals leads us not only to a heightened appreciation of human intellect and reason but also to a deeper recognition of God's hand in creation. The Roman Catholic Church has long held that faith and reason are not antagonistic but complementary. Within this framework, the universals we discern through philosophical inquiry are harmonized with the divine truths revealed through faith. The clearer we see these universals, the clearer we recognize the divine architecture of which we are a part.

In this regard, universals are not mere abstractions or artifacts of linguistic convenience but are essential to our understanding of the world and our place within it. They guide us towards higher truths and ethical conduct, acting as beacons in our intellectual and spiritual journey. As such, they serve both as evidence of a designed cosmos and as invitations to delve deeper into the mystery of existence, ultimately pointing us towards the divine and the Church that guards these ultimate truths.

By contextualizing universals within the grand narrative of creation, we find ourselves not only philosophically enriched but also spiritually compelled. The patterns and principles that unite diverse realms of knowledge act as signposts, guiding humanity towards a unity that mirrors the oneness of their divine source. The universals prompt us to move beyond mere academic interest, urging a return to the underlying source of all being.

In our journey through the philosophical terrain of universals, we see that the harmony of abstract concepts reflects a higher cosmic order. This chapter thus serves as a bridge to further discussions on comparative analysis and the role of faith and reason, elucidating how these universal principles underpin a coherent, theologically grounded worldview. The universals don't merely exist in the abstract; they draw us to realize an intelligent and purposeful design, ultimately leading us back to the divine architect – God, whose Church holds the key to comprehending these universals in their fullest sense.

Key Philosophical Concepts

Philosophy often engages with the fundamental questions that underpin reality, knowledge, and existence. Central to this is the understanding that certain concepts, termed universals, persist across various philosophical traditions and schools of thought. These universals are not random but are signposts guiding humanity toward an acknowledgment of divine creation and, ultimately, the path leading to the Roman Catholic Church.

One of the cornerstone concepts in philosophy is *being*. It's the inquiry into what it means to "be" or to exist. Martin Heidegger called this the "question of being" and it has profound implications. In Catholic thought, this is amplified through the understanding that existence itself is a gift from God. God is described as "He Who Is," encapsulating the profound belief that God is the ultimate source of all being. This cornerstone provides a metaphysical grounding that aligns with the Church's teachings on the nature of existence and the Creator.

Truth is another key concept. Philosophers from ancient Greece to modern times have debated what truth is and how it can be known. The Roman Catholic

Church teaches that ultimate truth is revealed by God and is found wholly in Jesus Christ, who said, "I am the way, the truth, and the life." This objective truth transcends individual perception and aligns with the universal laws seen across disciplines, such as mathematics and science, pointing to a coherent, divinely ordered universe.

Moreover, the concept of **goodness** weaves through philosophical discussions as not just moral righteousness but as an intrinsic quality desired by all. Aristotle's notion of the "good life" or "eudaimonia" fits seamlessly into the Catholic vision of living virtuously. Goodness, in the Church's doctrine, reflects God's nature, implying that virtuous living is not merely a human endeavor but a participation in divine life. This universal quest for goodness among humans underscores a divine blueprint, suggesting that our moral codes are set by a higher power.

The concept of justice further elucidates these philosophical universals. Justice is typically understood as giving each their due and is a cornerstone in Plato's "Republic." The Church elevates this by emphasizing divine justice, which harmonizes mercy and fairness. God's justice ensures that while human justice may falter, divine justice prevails, affirming that our human systems are reflections, albeit imperfect, of a heavenly order.

In the realm of **beauty**, Plato's ideals are epitomized through the Church's view on splendor and sacred art. St. Thomas Aquinas posited that beauty comprises wholeness, harmony, and radiance, which can manifest in both the cosmos and created art. This belief mirrors the Church's dedication to architecture, liturgy, and music as reflections of divine beauty. The appreciation of beauty, therefore, extends beyond mere sensory experience. It is perceived as an encounter with the divine, nudging the soul toward its Creator.

The examination of **the one and the many** also remains pivotal in philosophical discussions and aligns profoundly with Catholic theology. The tension between unity and diversity in the world reflects the inherent unity of God as the ultimate source, while the variety of His creation showcases His infinite creativity. This philosophical universal finds its culmination in the doctrine of the Trinity which, while being one in essence, exhibits a mysterious plurality of persons.

Causality, another integral concept, often encapsulated in the principle of cause and effect, aligns with philosophical arguments for God's existence, notably Aquinas's Five Ways. Every effect in nature necessitates a cause, and ultimately, a first cause. For Catholics, God is the First Cause, an unmoved mover who set the universe into being. This paramount philosophical concept aligns with the Church's understanding of God as Creator and sustainer of all that exists.

Exploring the concept of **free will** delves into the Catholic Church's teaching about human dignity and moral responsibility. Philosophers have long debated the extent of human freedom, a debate that spans from determinism to existentialism. Catholic teaching, however, upholds that while God's providence governs the universe, human beings are endowed with free will to choose good or evil. This not only emphasizes human autonomy but also underscores the moral responsibility inherent in our choices, inviting a deeper understanding of sin and virtue.

Lastly, the notion of *teleology* infuses much of philosophical thought— the study of purpose and design in the universe. Aristotle's final cause and Aquinas's eventual causes elucidate that everything in nature has a purpose, a view that Catholicism elevates. The Church teaches that all creation is directed towards a purpose — to glorify God and attain eternity with Him. This purposive design of the universe, therefore, is an imprint of divine intention and wisdom.

Thus, key philosophical concepts such as being, truth, goodness, justice, beauty, unity, causality, free will, and teleology not only unite disparate branches of human thought but also highlight a divinely inspired coherence. These universals serve as philosophical signposts leading humanity toward an understanding of a divine architect — a Creator whose magnificence and wisdom find their fullest expression in the doctrines and teachings of the Roman Catholic Church. Each concept nudges us closer to acknowledging the intrinsic order and divine purpose infused by God into the very fabric of reality. Thus, embracing these philosophical universals becomes not just an intellectual exercise but a spiritual journey toward the heart of God's Church.

Arguments for a Divine Architect

In contemplating the grand tapestry of our existence, one invariably encounters mysteries that beg the question of an underlying intelligence. This section seeks not merely to assert but to elucidate the compelling arguments for the presence of a Divine Architect, one whose intricate designs are evident in the very fabric of our universe. While numerous philosophical universals can be scrutinized as potential proofs, particularly compelling is the intricacy with which various disciplines—mathematics, science, and metaphysics—interweave and harmonize. The very coherence and structured complexity found within these realms suggest an intelligent source beyond mere chance or random chaos.

Firstly, consider the precision with which universal constants govern our physical world. Constants such as the gravitational constant, the speed of light, and Planck's constant seem finely tuned to facilitate life. Even the slightest deviation in these values would render the universe uninhabitable. This fine-tuning suggests a calibrating hand—one that not only constructed the laws of physics but also set them into a precise balance to foster life. This concept aligns with the teleological argument, which posits that the order and efficiency apparent in natural systems imply intentional design.

Moving from the realm of physics to that of biology, the human body's integrated systems offer a further illustration of divine craftsmanship. The mutual dependence of our circulatory, nervous, and respiratory systems indicates a level of design complexity that surpasses simple evolutionary adaptation. While evolution explains aspects of our physiological development, the holistic integration and synchronicity of these systems hint at an orchestrated plan, an intelligent blueprint that accounts for their co-dependence from the outset.

We must also note the ubiquitous presence of mathematical universals. Mathematical constants and geometrical principles appear consistently throughout nature, from the spiral patterns of galaxies to the symmetrical beauty of snowflakes. The universality of these principles suggests a blueprint—a set of rules under which the universe operates. Mathematics serves as the language of this divine architect, enabling humanity to decode and understand the cosmos. This realization has prompted philosophers such as René

Descartes and mathematicians like Pythagoras to argue for the preexistence of mathematical forms in the divine intellect.

The anthropic principle further strengthens the argument for a Divine Architect. This principle posits that the universe appears tailored to accommodate conscious beings who can ponder its vastness and, more importantly, recognize its intricate design. The conditions necessary for life are so specific and rare that their convergence seems statistically improbable under a random, unguided process. The fact that we exist in a universe capable of fostering life increasingly leans towards intelligent design rather than fortuitous accident.

From the perspective of metaphysics, we encounter the argument of necessity and contingency. Everything in our observable universe is contingent; it relies on something else for its existence. This chain of contingency, philosophers argue, must ultimately trace back to a necessary being that exists independently and initiates the existence of all else. This necessary being, unchanged and eternal, aligns with the concept of God in classical theism. Within Roman Catholic thought, this line of reasoning is most famously developed in

Aquinas's Five Ways, particularly the argument from contingency.

Ethical universals also serve as a profound testament to the existence of a moral architect. Across cultures, certain moral principles—such as the inherent wrongness of murder or the virtue of compassion—remain remarkably consistent. This global ethical resonance suggests the presence of a moral lawgiver, an entity that imbued humanity with an intrinsic understanding of right and wrong. The objectivity of these moral truths defies relativistic interpretations and points instead to a divine source from which they emanate.

The laws of nature, too, are indicative of a governing intellect. The immutable properties of natural laws suggest regulation by a rational mind rather than serendipity. In this light, the natural world becomes a testament to a logical, ordered creator. The periodic table, for instance, manifests an elegant organization that reveals a deep-seated order in chemical substances, indicating a preordained structure that transcends human discovery.

Furthermore, the very act of human reasoning itself can be viewed as evidence of a Divine Architect. Our capacity for abstract thought, logical analysis, and philosophical reflection presupposes the intelligibility of the universe. This mutual intelligibility between the human mind and the cosmic order implies a shared origin—an act of creation that endowed humanity with cognitive faculties capable of deciphering the creator's grand design.

Cosmological arguments also lend substantial weight to the thesis of a Divine Architect. The Big Bang theory postulates a singular beginning to our universe, raising questions about what—or who—set it into motion. The notion of a timeless, spaceless cause that is powerful enough to bring a universe into existence aligns with the characteristics of the deity in Roman Catholic teachings. This initial cause, devoid of temporal and spatial constraints, fits the description of an omnipotent creator.

Beyond these logical and empirical proofs, the experiential dimension cannot be overlooked. Throughout history, individuals have recounted encounters with the divine—a sense of connection with an overarching intelligence that transcends empirical verification. While skeptics may dismiss these experiences as mere psychological phenomena, the transformative power and consistency of these testimonies across cultures and eras suggest contact with a genuine source of transcendence.

In sum, the arguments for a Divine Architect converge from multiple disciplines, each revealing a layer of the grand design. Whether through the precision of physical constants, the complexity of biological systems, the universality of mathematical principles, or the moral intuitions embedded in the human spirit, the evidence for an intelligent designer is compelling. These converging lines of reasoning affirm the presence of a creator whose ultimate purpose, as the Roman Catholic Church teaches, is to lead humanity into a relationship with Him—a relationship that finds its fullness within the embrace of the Church.

Chapter 9: Comparative Analysis

The intricate tapestry of our physical and metaphysical existence reveals its profound complexities when we delve into various disciplines. Each field, be it scientific, philosophical, or theological, presents a unique perspective, yet there lies an undeniable convergence of ideas. This chapter aims to dissect these convergences, underscoring the Roman Catholic Church's unique position in bridging these realms. Our comparative analysis illuminates how universal structures in nature, human cognition, and divine revelation are intertwined, presenting a coherent narrative that exalts God as the creator, ultimately leading all to His Church.

To commence, consider the structural concepts shared across disciplines. The cornerstone of these concepts lies in their universal nature; whether observable in the periodic table or discernible in philosophical truths, the pattern is unmistakable. When we observe the periodic table's arrangement, it is more than a mere catalog of elements. It is a quintessential example of ordered complexity, where each element has its place and function. This mirrors the liturgical calendar of the Roman Catholic Church, where each feast and season serves a specific spiritual purpose, contributing to the overarching harmony.

One cannot ignore the synchronicity between the integrated systems of the human body and the hierarchical yet interdependent structure of the Church. The body's systems, from the cardiovascular to the nervous, operate in unison to sustain life, analogous to the combined roles of sacraments, liturgies, and ecclesiastical authorities in sustaining spiritual life within the Church. Whether we focus on the heart pumping blood or the Eucharist nourishing the soul, the parallels are striking and illuminate a divine blueprint.

Examining the universe, we note significant similarities in the forces governing celestial bodies and the moral laws that guide human conduct. Fundamental forces like gravity and electromagnetism are as essential for the cosmos as the commandments are for moral order. This juxtaposition underlines that just as the cosmos requires precision and balance, so does human behavior, as taught by the Church. The celestial arrangements point to a designer who is both meticulous and omnipotent, advocating for an ordered existence that the Catholic doctrine epitomizes.

Mathematical universals serve as another point of comparison. The elegance of mathematical theorems and theorems' truths make them almost transcendent, elevating our contemplation of divine order. The Pythagorean theorem, Euler's identity, and prime numbers are more than proofs; they are manifestations of the divine intellect. These principles resonate with the Church's dogmas, which offer timeless, transcendent truths beyond empirical reach. Both mathematics and faith call for belief in unseen realities, substantiated by reason and experience.

The scientific endeavor, too, reveals the invisible hand of the creator. Laws of physics, from Newtonian mechanics to quantum theory, portray a universe bound by consistent principles. This consistency is mirrorod in tho thoologioal dootrinoo of tho Churoh, which provide an unchanging moral and spiritual framework. Just as scientists rely on reproducible results and laws to understand nature, so do believers look to tradition and scripture to comprehend their faith. These correlations affirm that the search for truth, be it scientific or spiritual, leads to a recognition of a higher power.

Philosophical universals also converge on the idea of a divine architect. The ontological arguments for God's existence, as posited by Anselm and later refined by Descartes, urge us to consider that the very concept of a supreme being dictates its existence. Likewise, the moral arguments from Kant and Aquinas emphasize a lawgiver behind the moral laws inscribed in the human conscience. The philosophical quest for ultimate causes and principles aligns seamlessly with the theological assertions of the Catholic Church, revealing a unified framework for understanding reality.

Impacting human understanding, these comparative analyses foster a sense of unity and purpose. Recognizing the Church's teachings reflected in natural laws and intellectual endeavors encourages a harmonious view of existence. By appreciating these universal structures, individuals can better perceive their place in the divine plan. This not only enhances intellectual exploration across disciplines but also enriches spiritual insight, leading skeptics and believers alike toward a greater truth.

The capacity to draw connections between disparate fields and discover common threads points to an underlying order. This order, far from being a product of random evolution, suggests a designer who orchestrates every detail. The Roman Catholic Church's role is thus not just a custodian of faith but also a beacon of truth, guiding humanity towards recognizing the divine in every aspect of life. The comparative analysis serves as a testament to the Church's unique mission, standing at the intersection of faith, reason, and universal harmony.

Indeed, the Roman Catholic Church is uniquely positioned to elucidate these intersections. Its rich intellectual tradition, encompassing the works of Augustine, Aquinas, and countless others, presents a cohesive worldview where science, philosophy, and theology are not isolated disciplines but integrated pathways to truth. This comprehensive approach underscores the Church's commitment to exploring and revealing the divine imprints in all facets of existence.

As we conclude this comparative analysis, it becomes evident that the universality of truth is a hallmark of divine creation. The Roman Catholic Church, through its doctrines, traditions, and teachings, encapsulates this universality. By aligning scientific understanding with theological wisdom and philosophical inquiry, the Church reveals the divine blueprint woven into the very fabric of existence. This revelation calls all individuals, regardless of their initial vantage point, to a deeper recognition of God as the creator and to ultimately find their spiritual home in His Church.

In essence, the comparative analysis not only highlights the Church's role in uniting various domains of knowledge but also invites a profound contemplation of our existence. It beckons us to transcend mere academic pursuit and recognize the spiritual dimension that underpins all. Thus, our exploration of universal structures across different disciplines points back to a singular origin and end: a divine harmony orchestrated by God, leading all into the fold of His Roman Catholic Church.

Similarities in Structural Concepts

At first glance, the Roman Catholic liturgical calendar, the periodic table of elements, and various scientific laws may appear to be disparate. However, under closer examination, they reveal deep structural similarities that underscore the magnificence of a unified, divine architecture. These similarities are not merely superficial but penetrate the underlying frameworks that govern natural and spiritual realms.

The structured nature of the Roman Catholic liturgical calendar, with its rhythm of feasts, solemnities, and ordinary times, is a beautiful representation of order. This divine order mirrors the systematic arrangement found within the periodic table of elements. Both systems serve as blueprints in their respective domains—one guiding spiritual formation, the other providing foundational principles in the physical sciences.

The periodic table, developed through meticulous scientific inquiry, exhibits a remarkable order among various elements. This order is not arbitrary but reflects an intrinsic harmony in the universe. Elements are grouped based on their properties, revealing patterns that speak to an underlying purpose. Similarly, the Roman Catholic liturgical calendar orders the sacred year in a way that guides the faithful through the mysteries of Christ's life and the seasons of faith, suggesting a spiritual periodicity orchestrated by a divine hand.

In exploring both, one notes the principles of recurrent themes and patterns. The periodic table's groups and periods resonate with the cyclical nature of the liturgical calendar. Just as elements exhibit recurring properties in specific groups, so too do the liturgical seasons recur annually, reinforcing core aspects of the faith. This highlights an intrinsic propensity for order that exists both in spiritual and material realities.

Turning our attention to the human body, we see another layer of this divine structuring. The human body's various systems—nervous, circulatory, and respiratory—integrate seamlessly to maintain life. Each system is critically interdependent on the others, resembling the interdependence seen within elements of the periodic table and the interconnected seasons within the liturgical year. The same intricate designs permeate our biology, implying a common creative force.

Scientific theorems and laws further display this divine structuring. Newton's laws of motion and thermodynamics, for instance, exhibit a precision that governs every physical interaction. Their predictability and consistency point back to a deliberate and intelligent source. In much the same way, the theological doctrines and rhythms of the Roman Catholic Church remain constants providing spiritual guidance, operating under a set of divine principles safeguarded through tradition and scripture.

In mathematics, the Fractal Geometry offers another dimension of this structural congruence. Fractals reveal how complex patterns emerge from simple rules, similar to how profound spiritual truths navigate from basic liturgical practices. The repetitive nature of fractal patterns evokes the recurring liturgical seasons, underscoring the might of universal laws applicable both to natural phenomena and spiritual theology.

Further probing into the philosophical universals, one finds that key concepts across different philosophical systems often converge on the idea of a harmoniously ordered cosmos. Classical philosophers like Aristotle and Aquinas spoke of a prime mover and an intelligent designer, beliefs that underpin both the systematic laws observed in science and the sacred rhythms governing the Church's liturgical practices. Each discipline seeks to understand and express this underlying order in its own language, reaffirming the existence of a deliberate, intelligent architect.

One might wonder, why such a concerted effort across these various fields? The answer is simple yet profound: they all reveal a structure that aims to draw humanity closer to an understanding and appreciation of divine order. Whether it's through the predictable patterns of nature, the cadences of the liturgical year, or the logical consistency found in scientific principles, every domain whispers the existence of an overarching divine narrative.

This deeply integrated perspective not only harmonizes our understanding of the universe but also elevates the Roman Catholic Church as the vessel chosen to foster, nurture, and disseminate this divine wisdom. It acts as both a conduit and custodian of a universal truth intricately embedded in the fabric of reality and echoed through the realms of science, nature, and human understanding.

In recognizing the presence of similarities in structural concepts between these seemingly unrelated domains, we begin to appreciate the cohesive marvel of creation. These reflections invite believers to see the Creator's hand in every part of life and encourage skeptics to ponder the possibility of an intelligently designed universe. It calls upon scientists and philosophers alike to reassess their understandings, employing both reason and faith to grasp the full beauty of an interconnected cosmos.

Indeed, the structural similarities across disciplines signify more than coincidence. They point towards a unified theory of divinity—a testament to the Roman Catholic Church's assertion of an orderly, purposeful, and divine creation designed to lead all into God's grand design. Whether through the divine rhythm shown in sacred liturgies or the mathematical precision reflected in scientific laws, all roads converge towards an exaltation of the greatest architect—the Creator Himself.

Impact on Human Understanding

How does the intricate design of the universe shape our understanding of existence? This is not just a question for philosophers and theologians but also for scientists, educators, and the common person seeking meaning. The Roman Catholic Church posits that the harmony and order found in universal structures are not random; they are deliberate signals leading us toward the divine.

In exploring the comparative analysis of these universals, one immediately notices the extraordinary consistency across different fields. Whether one is examining the cyclical nature of the Liturgical Calendar or the symmetrical beauty in the Periodic Table of Elements, there's a recurring theme of order and purpose. This alignment across various disciplines compels us to rethink the notion of mere coincidence, pushing us to consider a grand designer behind all creation.

The impact on human understanding is monumental. When we realize that the same principles governing the cosmic arrangements of elements also align with the theological underpinnings of faith, something clicks in our collective psyche. It's as if the universe is a grand symphony and, for the first time, we're hearing its melody clearly. This clarity can bridge the gap between skeptical inquiry and religious conviction, allowing for a more unified approach to knowledge and belief.

The Roman Catholic Church finds profound validation in this comparative analysis. The structure and order evidenced in nature mirror the Church's liturgical structure, sacraments, and teachings. This mirroring serves as a sort of divine fingerprint, affirming the Church's role as a vessel of God's truth. The very fact that we can draw parallels between the structure of atoms and the sacrosanct rituals observed for centuries underscores a universal language crafted by God. This universality reinforces the Church's claim that it is meant for all of humanity, irrespective of different cultural or intellectual backgrounds.

By studying these universals in a comparative framework, we also expand our intellectual horizons. For instance, the integrated systems of the human body aren't just biological marvels but metaphors for spiritual interconnectedness. Each system, from the cardiovascular to the nervous, works harmoniously, suggesting that our spiritual lives, too, need a harmonious balance for optimal well-being. Such comparative analysis allows us to appreciate the full spectrum of human experience, from the physical to the metaphysical.

Moreover, the impact extends to the realm of education. When educators highlight these universal structures in their teaching, they are doing more than imparting knowledge—they are instilling a sense of wonder and purpose. Students, whether they're in scientific fields or theological studies, begin to see the interconnectedness of all things. This realization can inspire future generations to seek knowledge not just for its own sake but for the greater purpose of understanding our place in the divine plan.

For scientists, this comparative analysis acts as a fulcrum, tilting perspectives from empiricism to existential queries. When scientific laws and theorems exhibit a divine order, it nudges scientists to acknowledge possibilities beyond material explanations. This slight shift doesn't diminish the rigor of scientific inquiry; instead, it enhances it by adding a layer of depth and humility. Recognizing a potential divine architect doesn't undermine scientific endeavors but enriches them by placing them in a grander narrative.

For philosophers, the exploration of universal structures across various domains offers a rich tapestry for existential and epistemological debates. The orderly nature of the cosmos, the periodicity observed in natural laws, and the intricate design evident in biological systems provide fertile ground for arguing the existence of a divine planner. These arguments serve as philosophical bridges reconciling reason with belief, offering a holistic view of reality.

This understanding also transforms the skeptics. A comparative analysis of universal structures doesn't merely preach to the choir; it reaches out to those standing on the fringes of faith. Skeptics are often swayed by empirical evidence and logical reasoning. By showcasing the undeniable patterns and consistencies across disciplines, the analysis speaks to their logical faculties. It plants seeds of curiosity, prompting an honest re-evaluation of the stance that all is random and purposeless.

The overall human understanding, therefore, benefits immensely. By recognizing the divine hand in the universals, we foster a culture that values both faith and reason. This dual appreciation enriches our lives, giving them depth and direction. Instead of seeing science and religion as opposing forces, we begin to see them as two lenses focusing on the same truth from different angles. This holistic understanding paves the way for a more integrated approach to solving the world's most pressing issues, lifting human civilization towards greater harmony and purpose.

Thus, the impact on human understanding is not merely academic or confined to intellectual debates. It permeates every aspect of life, from our educational systems to our spiritual practices, influencing both personal growth and collective evolution. By acknowledging the divine orchestration behind universal structures, humanity stands on the cusp of a transformative renaissance, one that harmonizes the best of faith, reason, and empirical evidence.

As we delve deeper into these comparative analyses, we recognize that the ultimate goal is not just to identify patterns but to understand their significance. This understanding acts as a guiding light, leading us toward the Roman Catholic Church, where these universal truths find their fullest expression. By embracing this knowledge, we open ourselves to a life of greater meaning, purpose, and divine alignment.

The path is clear: we must continue to explore, analyze, and reflect upon these profound connections. Only then can we fully appreciate the divine blueprint laid before us, guiding humanity toward its true destiny as intended by God.

Chapter 10: The Role of Faith and Reason

Faith and reason have often been portrayed as opposing forces, but history paints a different picture. In the context of rational inquiry, faith is not a blind leap into the dark but a light that illuminates the path of understanding. Roman Catholicism has long held that faith and reason are complementary principles that, when embraced together, lead to a fuller comprehension of the universe and our place within it. This synergistic relationship is evident across centuries of theological and scientific advancements.

The Catholic Church teaches that faith without reason can devolve into superstition, while reason without faith risks becoming sterile and dehumanizing. This harmonious balance is not merely theoretical but practical—it has guided the Church through epochs of intellectual flourishing. St. Thomas Aquinas, for instance, masterfully integrated Aristotelian philosophy with Christian doctrine, creating an enduring framework wherein theological truths and rational principles coexist. This intellectual tradition continues to be a bastion of Catholic thought, urging us to see God in the logic and order of the world.

Scientific inquiry, driven by reason, often leads to profound encounters with the mysteries of creation—mysteries that beckon for faith. When a scientist peers through a telescope and witnesses the vastness of the cosmos, or when a biologist uncovers the intricate complexity of cellular life, the impulse to ask "why" naturally arises. These questions echo through the annals of both science and religion, seeking answers that neither discipline can fully provide in isolation. It is here that faith steps in, providing meaning when reason reaches its limit.

Moreover, the role of faith is essential in the moral dimension of scientific exploration. As we unlock the secrets of the universe, ethical considerations come to the forefront—questions about how new knowledge should be applied for the greater good. The Roman Catholic Church offers a moral compass grounded in centuries of philosophical and theological wisdom, guiding scientists and laypeople alike to use their findings in a manner that honors God's creation.

In the grand symphony of existence, reason and faith are not solo instruments battling for dominance; they are harmonizing elements of a divine composition. As we continue to explore the realms of science and philosophy, let us do so with both reason and faith as our guides, recognizing that every discovery is a note in the larger symphony orchestrated by the Creator.

Faith in the Context of Rational Inquiry

In the quest for understanding the mysteries of existence, one often encounters the timeless debate between faith and reason. For many, these two concepts appear as polar opposites, locked in an eternal struggle. However, upon closer examination, it becomes evident that this dichotomy is a false one. Faith and reason, far from being adversaries, are complementary forces that together illuminate a more profound truth. This section explores the intricate relationship between faith and rational inquiry, showcasing how they unite to lead us toward a deeper grasp of the divine.

Throughout history, the Roman Catholic Church has stood as a beacon of this harmonious relationship. The Church's scholars and theologians have long asserted that faith need not reject reason, nor should reason dismiss faith. Instead, they argue, faith elevates reason, bringing it into the realm of the divine, where human understanding alone cannot reach. St. Thomas Aquinas, perhaps one of the most famous proponents of this view, rigorously articulated that faith and reason are both necessary to grasp the fullness of truth.

Rational inquiry, grounded in observable phenomena and logical processes, offers us a structured method for comprehending the world around us. The scientific method, a crowning achievement of human intellect, has unveiled the wonders of the cosmos, the intricacies of biological life, and the profound laws of mathematics. These discoveries offer a glimpse of the divine architect at work, as the intricate design and order in the universe resonate with the notion of an intelligent creator. Indeed, it would be an impoverished view to consider these marvels as mere coincidences, devoid of any higher purpose.

Faith steps in where reason reaches its limits. It provides the moral and spiritual framework that gives meaning to the discoveries of science and philosophy. Faith doesn't just fill gaps in our empirical knowledge; rather, it transcends it, offering a fuller picture of reality that includes the spiritual and the eternal. Through faith, the truths uncovered by reason are imbued with deeper significance, pointing us toward a divine origin.

Consider the example of the periodic table of elements. This elegant display of empirical knowledge reveals not just the building blocks of matter, but the incredible order that governs them. Faith allows us to see this order not just as an accident of nature, but as a deliberate design by a wise and benevolent Creator. The compatibility of such knowledge with faith is a testament to the Church's assertion that true scientific inquiry ultimately leads us closer to understanding God.

The relationship between faith and reason also finds expression in the natural law, a key concept in Catholic theology. Natural law posits that the universe operates according to certain principles that are both knowable through human reason and inherently aligned with divine will. The study of natural law demonstrates how moral truths are accessible to all, regardless of religious background, thereby uniting humanity through a shared rational and moral framework.

It's essential to acknowledge the role of skepticism in this dialogue. Skepticism urges caution and demands rigorous proof, pushing the boundaries of both faith and reason. In this sense, skepticism acts as a refining fire, purifying and strengthening our convictions. The Church's rich tradition of philosophical inquiry is, in part, a response to skepticism, demonstrating that faith is not blind belief but a reasoned trust in truths that transcend empirical evidence.

Moreover, the harmony between faith and reason is not limited to abstract concepts; it is evident in the lives of individuals. Saints and scholars alike have embodied this union. Figures like St. Augustine and St. Teresa of Avila exemplify how deep faith can inspire rigorous intellectual pursuit and vice versa. Their lives are testaments to the belief that reason, far from undermining faith, can actually serve to deepen it.

In the context of contemporary science, discoveries in physics, biology, and cosmology often raise questions that touch on the divine. The fine-tuning of the universe, the origin of life, and the complexity of the human mind all point to realities that seem to invite theological reflection. Faith allows scientists and scholars to perceive these enigmas not as random occurrences, but as part of a purposeful and coherent whole designed by a Creator.

The philosopher and the theologian, the scientist and the believer, all find a place within the Roman Catholic Church that values both faith and reason. The Church, with its vast intellectual tradition, offers a unique perspective that transcends the limitations of a purely secular or purely religious view. By fostering an environment where questioning is encouraged and faith is nurtured, the Church stands as a testament to the belief that true understanding of the universe requires both rational inquiry and spiritual insight.

In conclusion, faith and rational inquiry are not mutually exclusive pursuits but are interwoven strands of the same tapestry, guiding us towards the ultimate truth. The Roman Catholic Church, through its teachings and traditions, exemplifies this harmonious relationship, asserting that true knowledge of creation, and indeed of the Creator, is reached through the synthesis of both faith and reason. As we delve deeper into the mysteries of existence, it becomes increasingly clear that this union enriches our understanding and draws us closer to the divine.

Harmonizing Science and Religion

One might imagine that science and religion, especially within the context of Roman Catholicism, are two realms destined never to meet. This perceived chasm is more nuanced and intricate than initially conceived. It's imperative to note that both science and religion seek truth, albeit through different methodologies. The Roman Catholic Church, historically and presently, posits that these domains are not merely complementary but harmoniously interwoven.

First, let's examine the inherent mission within both disciplines. Science endeavors to uncover the natural world's laws, decoding the universe's physical and biological elements. Religion, on the other hand, seeks to understand the divine, attributing purpose and meaning to life and existence. The Church posits that God, being the ultimate architect, fused these two pursuits into a coherent tapestry where investigating nature is akin to studying the handiwork of the Creator. Pope John Paul II eloquently expressed this concordance: "Science can purify religion from error and superstition; religion can purify science from idolatry and false absolutes."

In the medieval period, the Catholic Church wasn't merely an observer of scientific advancement but a pivotal player. Institutions like the University of Paris championed scholarly endeavors, bridging classical philosophy with theological insight. Scholars such as Thomas Aquinas synthesized Aristotelian logic with Christian doctrine, exemplifying the harmonious relationship between faith and reason. Aquinas' work in the Summa Theologica is foundational, asserting that faith and reason are not just compatible but symbiotic. He posited that reason could lead one to certain truths about God, while faith completes the picture, unveiling divine mysteries beyond human comprehension.

Still, skepticism persists among contemporary thinkers who view the Church's historical relationship with science as contentious. The Galileo affair is often cited, a period marked by the Church's initial resistance to heliocentric theories. Yet, upon closer scrutiny, this episode reveals much about the evolving understanding within the Church itself. It wasn't an outright denial of scientific pursuit but a cautious approach aligned with the theological framework of the time. Today, the Vatican sponsors astronomical research through the Vatican Observatory, symbolizing the ongoing commitment to scientific inquiry.

In the modern era, figures like Georges Lemaître, a Catholic priest, and physicist, revolutionized cosmology with the Big Bang theory, starkly illustrating that scientific discovery and religious vocation are not mutually exclusive. Lemaître's groundbreaking work echoes in cosmological studies, yet he remained steadfast in his faith, considering his scientific pursuits an exploration of God's creation. His dual profession as a scientist and clergy underscores a vital point: deep scientific inquiry can coexist and even fortify one's religious convictions.

Furthermore, the pursuit of scientific knowledge often prompts profound metaphysical questions that purely empirical methods can't address. These queries about the origin of the universe, the nature of consciousness, and the existence of moral laws often bleed into the philosophical and theological realms. Here, the Roman Catholic tradition offers a framework, suggesting that such profound questions find their answers in the divine character of God as revealed through Christ and the teachings of the Church. It's within this metaphysical discourse that science and religion intersect most compellingly.

The role of ethics in scientific advancement is another arena where the harmony between science and religion shines. The Church's moral teachings provide a vital compass guiding scientific research, especially with technologies such as genetic manipulation, artificial intelligence, and biotechnology. The encyclical "Laudato Si" by Pope Francis, which addresses ecological responsibility and sustainability, underscores that scientific and technological progress must be coupled with moral and ethical discernment. This perspective does not stifle innovation but engenders a holistic approach considering the welfare of humanity and creation.

Through the lens of faith, the enigmatic beauty and complexity of the universe aren't seen as mere byproducts of blind chance. Rather, they are evidence of an intelligent designer whose works inspire awe and wonder. The Catechism of the Catholic Church reinforces this: "Science and technology are precious resources when placed at the service of man and promote his integral development for the benefit of all." This statement encapsulates the Church's stance that scientific progress and religious belief are not adversaries but allies in the quest for truth and human flourishing.

The cumulative effect of these reflections demonstrates the depth of integration possible between science and religion. For the Catholic faithful, the universe's grandeur and the life within it echo the divine majesty. This perspective encourages the faithful, scientists among them, to engage with the world inquisitively and reverently, acknowledging that their scientific endeavors are a form of honoring the Creator.

Thus, harmonizing science and religion isn't just a philosophical endeavor but a practical reality, exemplified by the Church's commitment to educational institutions, research, and dialogue. This harmonization encourages a more profound exploration of truth that respects the nuances and insights offered by both faith and reason. Indeed, the journey to understanding the cosmos and our place within it is enriched by acknowledging the interplay of science and faith, both of which direct us toward the ultimate Creator of all.

Chapter 11: The Harmonious Design

The universe, with its vastness and complexity, constantly beckons us to ponder on the origins of its splendor. The fabric of the cosmos, from the tiniest particle to the grandest galaxy, is woven with such intricate precision that one cannot help but admire its harmonious design. The concept of Intelligent Design is not merely a philosophical notion or a theological assertion; it is evident in every facet of existence. But what does this harmony suggest to believers and skeptics alike?

Consider the meticulous structures within the natural world. Take, for instance, the Fibonacci sequence observable in the arrangement of leaves, the formation of seashells, and the branching of trees. These patterns aren't random. They signify a hidden order, a reflection of a grand design. This isn't just a set of isolated occurrences but a universal truth stitched into the very fabric of reality. For the believers, this is the signature of a Divine Architect, while for the skeptics, it provides a ground for introspection.

For centuries, thinkers, scientists, and theologians have marveled at the synchrony evident in creation. The orbits of planets, the laws of physics, and the principles of mathematics all point towards an intricate yet coherent system. They echo the sentiments articulated in Psalms, "The heavens declare the glory of God; the skies proclaim the work of his hands." When Sir Isaac Newton formulated the laws of motion, he wasn't just unearthing the mechanics of the universe. He was, in a sense, revealing the brushstrokes of the Creator.

Intelligent Design isn't restricted to grand cosmic scales alone. Let's narrow our focus to the microcosm, the cellular level of life. DNA, the blueprint of all living organisms, is composed of a mere four nucleotide bases. Yet, these bases combine in an almost infinite number of sequences to produce the vast diversity of life we witness. It is in the very language of life, written in these sequences, we find an eloquent testimony to purposeful creation.

Such intricacies extend beyond biological realms. They penetrate the principles of chemistry, physics, and beyond. For example, the specific properties of water, such as its unique density behavior, make life possible. Water's ability to expand upon freezing ensures that ice floats, insulating aquatic life during cold seasons. This seemingly simple yet critical feature underscores the argument for a thoughtful design.

These facets of Intelligent Design have profound implications for both believers and skeptics. Believers find in them an affirmation of their faith, a tangible manifestation of God's hand in every corner of the universe. For skeptics, the challenge is to explain away these signs of design as mere coincidences or products of natural selection. However, every discovery, from the double helix structure of DNA to the fine-tuning of the constants of physics, demands scrutiny.

What does this harmony teach us? Beyond spiritual or doctrinal affirmations, it introduces us to a universe that is fundamentally coherent and ordered. Mathematicians speak of "unreasonable effectiveness," where mathematical frameworks predict physical realities. This isn't just an academic curiosity; it's a testament to a consistent, universal order. Einstein once remarked that "the most incomprehensible thing about the world is that it is comprehensible." Indeed, this comprehensibility speaks volumes about the underlying harmonious design.

The implications of this harmony challenge every field of human inquiry. Whether one approaches the world through the lens of theology, science, or philosophy, the synchrony inherent in design offers a common ground. It is an invitation to marvel, to explore, and ultimately, to acknowledge that there might be more to existence than mere chance.

For the Roman Catholic Church, this harmonious design forms a cornerstone of its teachings. The Church posits that faith and reason coexist harmoniously, each illuminating the other. The universe, in its elegance and complexity, mirrors the divine, drawing humanity towards a deeper understanding of God. Hence, the exploration of natural phenomena becomes not just a scientific endeavor but also a spiritual journey. The Church has long upheld that truth is singular, whether derived from faith or reason, and that both streams lead to the Creator.

As we navigate through the realms of what we understand and what remains a mystery, the harmonious design of the universe stands as a beacon. It beckons us to probe further, to delve deeper into the symphony of existence. Whether we approach it from a religious conviction or a quest for empirical understanding, the end remains the same: awe and reverence for the grand tapestry that binds us all.

Every discovery in science, every philosophical insight, and every theological reflection, inevitably leads us back to the harmonious design. This is not just an abstract concept but a living reality, evident in the pulse of life and the expanse of the cosmos. It is a testament to an Intelligent Designer, a call to explore the universe with open hearts and minds. For believers, it reaffirms their journey of faith. For skeptics, it poses questions that defy simple answers, nudging them towards considering possibilities beyond the material.

In essence, the harmonious design of the universe serves as a bridge, connecting different realms of knowledge and belief. It invites all, irrespective of their starting point, to a unified understanding of existence. In this grand design, the Roman Catholic Church finds an affirmation of its faith, a guiding star leading to the Divine.

Evidence of Intelligent Design

The universe, with its myriad complexities and intricate structures, overwhelmingly suggests the presence of a Grand Designer. Scientists and philosophers alike have often marveled at the extraordinary specificity and balance required for life to exist. From the exact force of gravity to the unique properties of water, the evidence mounts, steadily pointing to an intelligent force behind it all. The mere probability of our universe having emerged by chance is near impossible. Such a staggering improbability does not merely suggest randomness but rather an underlying intentionality — an intelligent design.

Consider the fine-tuning argument, one that advocates that the constants of nature and the initial conditions of the universe must fall within an extraordinarily narrow range for life to exist. If gravitational force were slightly stronger or weaker, stars, planetary systems, and, ultimately, life as we know it could not exist. The precision with which these constants operate hints at a masterful orchestration — a divine symphony — rather than a fortuitous accident. Each force, each constant is precisely dialed, and the margin for error is practically nonexistent.

Furthermore, the specificity of universal constants extends beyond the physical to the biochemical. The complexity of DNA, the molecule of life, is another compelling piece of evidence. DNA is often described as a blueprint or code. This code is intricate, containing far more information than any man-made code or language. To think of DNA as occurring purely by chance diminishes the awe and reverence its complexity commands. Far from being a product of random processes, it points to an intelligent mind that authored it.

Additionally, the Anthropic Principle adds weight to the evidence of intelligent design. This principle posits that the universe's laws and constants appear finely-tuned for the existence of life, particularly human life. When viewed through the lens of the Roman Catholic faith, this principle takes on profound theological implications. It resonates with the belief that humanity is created in the image of God, and the universe is designed with a purpose: to be a home for humankind and, by extension, a realm for encountering the Divine.

Modern scientific discoveries, far from discrediting the notion of intelligent design, often reinforce it. Take, for instance, the discoveries in cosmology and particle physics. As researchers unveil the unfathomable complexities of the universe, from the macroscopic structures of galaxies to the microscopic intricacies of subatomic particles, a pattern of order and purpose emerges. It's as if the universe is written in the language of mathematics, a language that bespeaks design and intention, a language that aligns perfectly with the concept of a Divine Author.

Moreover, the harmony observed within natural laws points beyond mere functionality to something more profound – beauty. The laws of physics not only allow for the existence and sustenance of life, but they also exhibit a form of aesthetic elegance. This beauty, found both in the grandeur of the cosmos and the simplicity of a snowflake, speaks of a Creator who is not just a designer but an artist. The sheer symmetry and order we observe are not just practical but transcendently beautiful, underscoring a design that is both functional and awe-inspiring.

In addition to scientific observations, philosophical arguments also contribute to this discourse. The teleological argument remains one of the most potent philosophical defenses of intelligent design. This argument states that the presence of order and purpose in the world implies the existence of a purposeful Creator. The teleological perspective is not built on gaps in scientific knowledge, but rather on the presence of order and purpose where chaos might otherwise be expected.

Moreover, from a theological perspective, Sacred Scripture and the teachings of the Church are replete with affirmations of a universe purposefully created by God. The Church Fathers, spanning centuries, have echoed this view. St. Augustine, for instance, marveled at the order of creation and saw in it the handprint of God. Similarly, St. Thomas Aquinas' Five Ways offer logical arguments that demonstrate God's existence, with one way specifically dealing with the notion of intelligent design.

The implications of intelligent design extend deeply into the realm of ethics and morality. If the universe is designed with purpose, it follows that human life, too, has intrinsic meaning and value. This perspective fosters a deeper appreciation for human dignity and an innate sense of responsibility towards one another and creation. Within the Roman Catholic framework, this understanding is pivotal. It advances the notion that moral laws are not arbitrary but are reflections of a higher order, which is itself an expression of God's will.

Intelligent design is also a bridge for dialogue with skeptics and those from diverse intellectual traditions. Laypeople, scientists, and philosophers can find common ground in the awe and wonder elicited by the universe's complexity and fine-tuning. For those who may be skeptical of religious doctrines, the scientific and philosophical arguments for intelligent design can serve as a stepping stone towards a broader truth — a truth that ultimately leads to the acknowledgment of a Creator.

It's crucial, however, to differentiate intelligent design from simplistic creationism. What is advocated here is not an abandonment of scientific inquiry or an opposition to evolutionary theory. Instead, it is the acknowledgment that scientific facts, when viewed comprehensively, align with and even bolster the belief in an intelligent Creator. This synthesis of faith and reason is a hallmark of Roman Catholic thought and demonstrates the Church's commitment to understanding the truth through multiple lenses.

In conclusion, the evidence of intelligent design permeates through the fabric of reality, echoing a transcendent intelligence that intricately designed every facet of existence. From the foundational constants of the universe to the complex structure of DNA, from philosophical arguments to theological insights, every observation and reflection points to a purposeful creation. Such evidence not only enhances our understanding of the universe but also deepens our faith, underscoring the harmonious relationship between scientific discovery and divine revelation. Through this harmonious design, we find not just evidence but also a profound invitation — an invitation to marvel, to understand, and ultimately, to believe.

Implications for Believers and Skeptics

The Harmonious Design, as we've examined, stands as a testament to the exquisite interplay between faith and the empirical world. The implications of this intricate interweaving are profound, both for those who believe and for those who approach the universe with skepticism. Believers, whose faith is already attuned to seeing divine artistry in every facet of creation, find their convictions bolstered by the notion that every atom and theorem sings a note in a divinely orchestrated symphony. Conversely, skeptics are confronted with a compelling pattern that challenges their naturalistic assumptions, inviting a reconsideration of the metaphysical underpinnings of existence.

For believers, the harmonious design reaffirms the intimate connection between the material and the spiritual. It's a direct counter-narrative to the secular assertion that science and faith are mutually exclusive. The existence of universal constants and the fine-tuning of the cosmos suggest an architectural precision that transcends chance and coincidence. This alignment is far from an abstract concept; it offers tangible evidence that the universe is not a random assemblage of particles but a deliberate creation with purpose and intention behind every design choice. Thus, the design doesn't just align with, but profoundly enriches, their faith journey.

In essence, believers see the fingerprint of God in the precision and vastness of the cosmos. This perception is not confined to religious experiences; it permeates scientific inquiry, mathematics, and philosophical thought. When gazing at the periodic table or pondering the laws of physics, the devout are not merely observing order—they're witnessing God's continuous act of creation. It's a phenomenon that moves beyond just religious rites and sentiments; it integrates their entire experience of reality into a canvas painted by the Divine Artist.

Skeptics, on the other hand, are presented with a formidable puzzle. For many, the assumption has been that the universe's complexity is entirely the result of natural processes devoid of any intentional design. The harmonious design challenges this worldview by presenting evidence that can't be easily dismissed as mere happenstance. Observable patterns, mathematical constants, and the intricate balance within natural laws insinuate an underlying intelligence. While this does not irrefutably prove the existence of a divine creator, it undeniably opens the door to such a possibility, thus making materialism less absolute.

One critical implication for skeptics is the intellectual humility that the harmonious design demands. To acknowledge that there may be a metaphysical architect behind the physical constructs is to concede that human understanding is limited, and there is more to the cosmos than mere material interactions. This realization could pave the way for a more inclusive consideration of metaphysical explanations in scientific and philosophical discourses. In a broader sense, it underscores the possibility that empirical knowledge and spiritual insight are not competitors but complementary pursuits that together offer a fuller picture of reality.

Furthermore, the challenge for skeptics lies in reconciling the existence of intelligent design with the randomness that is often observed in nature. Naturalistic interpretations often rely on the premise that given enough time, complexity can spontaneously arise. However, the harmonious design posits that this complexity is so precisely ordered that attributing it to blind chance becomes increasingly untenable. Here lies the fascinating crossroads—whether one chooses to embrace the paradigm of a purposeful creator or continue in the quest to understand these phenomena under the umbrella of randomness and chaos theory.

To both believers and skeptics, the harmonious design points toward a shared human experience—a search for meaning and understanding in a seemingly infinite universe. For the philosophers and mathematicians among them, it pushes the boundaries of intellectual exploration, urging them to consider that the axioms and theorems they study might not just be abstract constructs but reflections of a grander divine intellect. It's a call to expand their intellectual inquiries to include theological dimensions, recognizing the potential divine craftsmanship in the matrices of their calculations and philosophies.

For scientists, it presents a paradigm where religious belief and scientific investigation are not mutually exclusive but rather mutually enriching. The acknowledgment of a harmonious design invites a deeper sense of wonder and curiosity about the natural world, transforming scientific pursuits into a form of worship. It encourages a synthesis of empirical rigor with spiritual depth, wherein every discovery is seen as a further unveiling of the Creator's mystery. It's an affirmation that faith can fuel scientific rigor, while science can deepen one's faith.

The implications extend into the realm of moral and ethical reflections as well. For believers, recognizing a deliberate design behind the universe reinforces the moral imperative to steward creation responsibly. The natural world, seen as a divine gift, comes with an inherent call to uphold and preserve its harmony. This perspective engenders a moral duty rooted in reverence and respect for God's creation. Believers are thus called to align their actions with this divine order, fostering a stewardship that reflects the harmony of the cosmos.

For skeptics, engaging with the harmonious design might lead to a reevaluation of ethical frameworks. If the universe is not merely a product of chance interactions but bears the mark of intelligent design, then human actions within it carry significant weight and responsibility. This shift in perspective could engender a more profound sense of accountability and purpose in human endeavors, encouraging a more ethical and conscientious approach to scientific and technological advancements.

Overall, the harmonious design serves as a bridge between disparate worldviews, inviting dialogue and reflection among diverse audiences. For the Roman Catholic Church, it offers a robust framework to articulate the compatibility of faith and reason, science and religion. It serves as an intellectual foundation upon which the Church can engage with contemporary scientific and philosophical discourses, demonstrating the relevance and profundity of its teachings in the modern world. The Church, thus, not only stands as a spiritual beacon but also as a thought leader that fosters meaningful conversations at the intersection of faith and empirical inquiry.

Ultimately, whether one is moved to deeper faith or intellectual curiosity, the harmonious design calls us to contemplate the profound order that underlies our existence. It prompts believers to see their faith not as a blind leap but as a reasoned trust in a purposeful creator. For skeptics, it poses the challenging but invigorating question of whether there is more to the universe than what meets the eye. In this interplay of belief and skepticism, a richer, more nuanced appreciation of the cosmos emerges—one that celebrates the unity of all knowledge under the auspices of divine wisdom.

Chapter 12: The Universal Call to the Roman Catholic Church

In contemplating the grand design of our universe, one is invariably led to perceive a singular orchestrator—God—and His chosen institution, the Roman Catholic Church. From the intricacies of the periodic table to the divine interplay of forces within the cosmos, every scientific and philosophical revelation beckons humanity to a deeper truth that surpasses mere academic inquiry. This universal call is not a mere whisper but a resounding proclamation of divine love and purpose, urging every individual—from the most skeptical scientist to the most devout philosopher—to recognize the Church as the fulcrum of truth and salvation. It is here, within the sacred tenets and sacramental life of the Roman Catholic Church, that the ultimate convergence of faith and reason is found, inviting all to embrace the divine architecture of existence.

Proofs of Divine Origin

Throughout the annals of history, humanity has sought to comprehend the divine. The profound complexity of this quest is encapsulated within the very fabric of the Roman Catholic Church. The Church stands not just as a pillar of faith but as an eternal testimony to divine orchestration. To understand the facets of its divine origin, an interdisciplinary approach can be instructive—merging theology, philosophy, mathematics, and science in a sublime blend that attests to an Intelligent Designer. This chapter seeks to illuminate how these wide-ranging universals all point towards the divine essence of the Roman Catholic Church.

The liturgical calendar of the Roman Catholic Church, for instance, is a beautiful manifestation of divine timing. Throughout different historical epochs, the Church's sacred traditions have remained remarkably consistent, offering a celestial blueprint that mirrors the grand design of the cosmos. Key seasons and feasts align rhythmically with the natural world, underscoring a synchrony that mere human invention could never achieve. Such synchronization hints at a divine architect who orchestrated not just the Church but the very nature of time itself.

Further evidence lies within the elemental foundations of our universe. The periodic table, with its precise arrangement, reflects an inherent order that transcends random chance. Each element's properties and relationships appear to be meticulously designed to support life and, by extension, the theological significance extending towards a higher purpose. The cosmic arrangements do more than sustain existence—they provide a reflective surface upon which divine handiwork can be seen. The fact that these elements are crucial for both physical existence and liturgical sacraments - from water in baptism to the fire representing the Holy Spirit - adds another dimension to their divine connections.

Turning to the intricate systems within the human body, one finds a similar signature of divine intentionality. The human form's integrated systems don't just reflect biological efficiency; they echo spiritual interconnectedness. The cardiovascular system's role in circulating blood—life itself metaphorically represented—brings to mind the Eucharist, where the blood of Christ nurtures the soul. Internally, our bodies reflect a sacred geometry, an intelligent design that finds its ultimate purpose in honoring the Creator.

Now, consider the fundamental forces governing our universe. Gravity, electromagnetism, the strong and weak nuclear forces all operate with such precision that physicists often remark on the 'fine-tuning' necessary for life. Within the context of Catholic theology, this isn't a mere coincidence. It signals the presence of a Creator whose invisible hand guides these forces to sustain a universe that leads souls towards divine truths. The theological implications of cosmology are vast, drawing an intrinsic link between the universe's physical laws and God's eternal wisdom.

Mathematics further showcases the hallmarks of a grand designer. Numbers and equations—immutable and universal—form the bedrock of understanding creation. Mathematical universals echo a divine order, making complex theorems and proofs not just intellectual exercises but spiritual pursuits. When mathematicians uncover a new theorem, they are, in a sense, gazing into the mind of God. The divine order seen in mathematics is yet another proof of an intelligent design that governs both the cosmos and the principles guiding the Roman Catholic Church.

Scientific laws, from Newton's laws of motion to Einstein's theory of relativity, elucidate the mechanisms of our physical world. These laws are not arbitrary; they display an elegant consistency that elevates natural phenomena to a form of divine poetry. When scientists decode these natural laws, they inadvertently unravel strands of God's grand narrative. This powerful evidence bolsters the Creator's invisible hand meticulously crafting a world that is both observable and knowable.

Philosophical universals apply another layer of understanding to this divine origin. Key philosophical concepts like metaphysics, ethics, and epistemology have their roots firmly planted in theological soil. The arguments for a divine architect, from Plato's Forms to Aquinas' Five Ways, reinforce the understanding that philosophy and theology are not opposed but are complementary pathways leading towards the same divine truth. These philosophical constructs align seamlessly with the teachings of the Church, further establishing its divine inception.

Yet, some might argue that these reflections are mere coincidences or products of human ingenuity. Comparative analysis across various structural concepts will reveal otherwise. When examined closely, the structural similarities in nature, science, and spirituality converge in ways that defy randomness. The harmonious design that permeates all creation calls for an Intelligent Designer, compellingly evidenced by the intricate and purposeful structures found within and outside the Church.

Resonating with humanity's inherent urge to seek truth, faith, and reason emerges as dual manifestations of God's guiding hand. Faith is not mere blind belief but a journey illuminated by rational inquiry. Harmonizing science and religion only strengthens the argument for divine origin, showcasing that rational thought and faith are not mutually exclusive but are co-pilots on the path to divine understanding. The symbiotic relationship between these realms portrays a masterful design, further making the case for the Church's divine origin.

Evidence of this intelligent design, as multifaceted as a beautifully cut diamond, shines in every domain from macrocosmic realms of the universe to the microcosmic complexities of DNA. For believers and skeptics alike, these proofs of divine origin operate as gentle yet mighty forces, guiding all towards acknowledging an all-encompassing truth: the presence of an intelligent, loving Creator who leads us all into the sanctity and grace of His Roman Catholic Church. The sublime orchestration witnessed in the universe takes its most profound expression in the framework of the Church, eternally inviting souls to partake in its divine embrace.

Leading All to God's Church

The notion of a universal call to the Roman Catholic Church is not merely a theological assertion; it resonates through every fiber of existence, from the cosmic to the cellular level. This idea permeates the intricate web of reality with such elegance that one can't help but stand in awe of its divine architect. The Church, as the sacred repository of truth, is envisioned to be the guiding beacon that illuminates the path for all humanity, aligning with a purpose that is intrinsically woven into the fabric of the universe.

What becomes strikingly apparent when one delves into various disciplines—whether it be physics, biology, mathematics, or even the abstract realms of philosophy—is the recurrent theme of unity and design. This unity is not a coincidence; it is a manifestation of divine will. The Roman Catholic Church, in its sacraments and teachings, reflects this cosmic unity. It is a living testament to the Creator's intent, a visible sign of an invisible grace that calls all to communion with God.

Historically, humanity has sought understanding in myriad ways, but it is within the Church that these disparate searchings find coherence. The teachings of the Church, grounded in centuries of tradition and theological reflection, provide a framework that unites these various strands of knowledge. From the Big Bang to the intricate dance of quarks, from the DNA helix to the periodic table, every element points back to a grand design that finds its fullest expression in God's Church.

Is it not wondrous how mathematical universals and scientific principles, which seem purely abstract and disconnected from spirituality, actually converge into a divine order? This convergence is not an accident. In the same way that mathematical theorems exhibit beauty and order, the doctrines of the Church resonate with the same inherent logic and grace. The sacraments and liturgies manifest the same structured elegance seen in the laws of nature.

Even skeptics, who might raise an eyebrow at the idea of a divine plan, often find themselves grappling with questions of purpose and meaning that lead invariably toward the same conclusions drawn by faith. Philosophers have long debated the existence of a higher power, often swinging between belief and doubt. However, the sheer harmony observed in the cosmos and our most sophisticated theories inevitably point to an underlying intelligence—a divine author whose narrative is precisely the story told by the teachings of the Roman Catholic Church.

Consider the abundant evidence in fields like cosmology and quantum mechanics, where the extraordinary precision in physical constants and laws defies the notion of random chance. The fine-tuning observed by scientists speaks volumes about an intentional design. Just as this argument for a Creator unfolds, so too does the Church unveil itself as the culmination of this divine wisdom, inviting all to partake in its sacramental life.

Faith and reason, often misconstrued as adversaries, are in fact complementary. When harmoniously interwoven, they reveal the splendor of God's creation and His Church. The doctrines of the Catholic faith offer a resolution to the existential questions that reason alone struggles to answer. It is in the Church that philosophy and science find their ultimate consummation, a realization that beckons all seekers of truth into its fold.

For the scientists, mathematicians, and philosophers who crave logical consistency and empirical evidence, the Roman Catholic Church presents an unparalleled synthesis of faith and reason. The Church's rich intellectual tradition, which includes luminaries like St. Thomas Aquinas and St. Augustine, demonstrates how reason and revelation collaborate in the quest for truth. It is through this lens that even the most skeptical minds can begin to see the patterns of divine orchestration.

Moreover, the role of the Church in fostering scientific inquiry throughout history cannot be overstated. Monastic communities preserved classical knowledge through the Dark Ages, and the patronage of the Church enabled the Renaissance. The Vatican Observatory, one of the oldest astronomical research institutions in the world, signifies the Church's commitment to scientific advancement. All these endeavors reflect the underlying belief that creation is comprehensible and that its beauty leads us inexorably to its Creator.

Evangelization, then, is not merely about preaching dogma; it is about unveiling the inherent truth embedded in all creation. By understanding and expounding on the universal structures found in various disciplines, the Church fulfills its mission to lead all to God. Whether through the precise harmonies of a Bach fugue or the elegant equations of Euler, each reveals a fragment of the divine narrative that ultimately points to the Church as the custodian of God's eternal truth.

The Church's teachings offer not just spiritual solace but intellectual fulfillment. It addresses the deepest longings of the human heart and mind. Through the liturgy and sacraments, it provides a tangible connection to the divine, affirming that all creation is sacramental and that the Creator's imprint is visible everywhere. The aesthetic and the rational converge in the Church's teachings, creating a holistic approach that meets both the soul's and the intellect's yearnings.

In conclusion, the universal call to the Roman Catholic Church is a call to come home to the ultimate truth, the ultimate beauty, and the ultimate good. This call reverberates through all aspects of the universe—the stars, the atoms, the theorems, the philosophical musings, and the spiritual reflections. Each beckons us towards a fuller understanding, which finds its consummation in the embrace of God's Church. This is the universal harmony, the divine symphony that invites all people from every walk of life to join in its everlasting hymn.

Conclusion

The journey through this text has been an exploration of the symphony that is creation, a symphony composed by none other than the Divine Composer. We traveled across multiple disciplines, from the intricacies of the human body to the cosmic arrangements of the periodic table, unveiling the underlying unity that points to one fundamental truth: God is the orchestrator of all universals. Despite the varying complexities and vast domains, a singular thread of intelligent design links everything from the most minute atomic particles to the grandeur of celestial bodies.

The Roman Catholic Church stands as the custodian of this divine wisdom, not just as a religious institution but as the epicenter of a cosmic revelation that resonates through history, science, philosophy, and mathematics. Historical perspectives have shown how the liturgical calendar and feasts are not mere rituals but symbols of cosmic significance. These traditions are imbued with layers of meaning that go beyond the spiritual, extending into the very fabric of reality.

Mathematics, often considered the purest form of logic and reason, does not escape the touch of the Divine.

The manifest precision in mathematical universals evidences a divine order, a meticulous design that underpins the world's complexity. Core theorems and proofs aren't just abstract concepts; they are reflections of a higher intelligence, providing a logical framework that aligns seamlessly with the beliefs held by the church.

Philosophical arguments further cement our understanding of this divine blueprint. The key concepts explored expose the intellectual rigor that supports the existence of a Divine Architect. The synthesis of these arguments with theological insights presents a compelling case for the divine origin of the universe and everything within it.

In presenting scientific theorems and laws, we reaffirmed the principle that faith and reason are not adversaries but complementary forces. The invisible hand of the Creator is evident, subtly guiding the principles that govern nature. From Newton's laws to Einstein's theories, scientific inquiry only deepens our wonder and reverence for the divine complexity woven into the universe.

The harmonious design evident in every facet of creation echoes the doctrine of intelligent design. Whether viewed through the lens of cosmology, biology, or philosophy, there is an undeniable order that challenges the randomness proposed by secular theories. This order beckons all, believers and skeptics alike, toward a greater understanding of a world purposefully arranged by a divine intelligence.

Through comparative analysis, it becomes clear that structural concepts across disciplines share remarkable similarities. These parallels are not coincidental but are deliberate patterns embedded by the Creator to facilitate human understanding. The convergence of these patterns in our study underscores the role of the Roman Catholic Church as a bridge between faith and reason, reconciling and harmonizing apparent contradictions.

Key to this exploration is the role of faith and reason in the pursuit of truth. Faith is not a blind leap but a rational assent to truths that reason discerns. The Catholic Church has always championed this harmony, exemplifying how faith enriches rational inquiry and vice versa. This synthesis is crucial in a world increasingly polarized between secularism and spirituality.

The universal call to the Roman Catholic Church emerges undeniably from the proofs and arguments presented. Regardless of one's starting point in this vast terrain of knowledge, all paths converge towards a singular truth - the divine origin leading to God's church. Every discovery in science, every philosophical insight, and every theological revelation points us to this ultimate union.

This conclusion is not the final note but an invitation to an ongoing symphony. Our exploration should compel us to further inquiry, deeper reflection, and more profound appreciation for the divine intricacies of our world. The Roman Catholic Church stands as a testament to this pursuit, guiding humanity towards a fuller understanding of the Creator and His creation.

In sum, let us embrace this harmonious design, recognizing the hand of God in the universals that bind our world. Let us approach the profundity of mathematical theorems, the complexity of biological systems, and the cosmic wonders with a sense of reverence and awe. And let our pursuit of knowledge always point us back to the ultimate source of all truth - God, who lovingly calls us into His Roman Catholic Church.

Appendix A: Appendix

In this appendix, we will delve into supplementary materials that enhance the understanding of the core arguments presented throughout this book. Contained herein are references, clarifications, and extended discussions that serve to underpin the assertions made in the chapters.

Additional References

The exploration of divine creation and intelligent design is supported by a myriad of scholarly works, theological texts, and scientific papers. Below is a curated list of key references that have been pivotal in shaping the dialogue between faith and reason:

- *Summa Theologica* by St. Thomas Aquinas

- *Cosmos* by Carl Sagan

- *The God Delusion* by Richard Dawkins (for counter-arguments)

- *Darwin's Doubt* by Stephen C. Meyer

- *Confessions* by St. Augustine

Terminology Clarifications

Given the diversity of the book's audience, it's crucial to clarify some terms that are used frequently:

- **Universal Structures:** These refer to foundational patterns or frameworks that are observable across different domains, such as science, philosophy, and theology.

- **Theological Implications:** This phrase explores how findings in various scientific and philosophical disciplines can be interpreted as evidence of divine orchestration.

- **Liturgy:** A form or formulary according to which public religious worship, especially Christian worship, is conducted.

Extended Discussions

Several concepts touched upon in this book warrant further exploration. Below are extended discussions and considerations:

- **The Symmetry of the Periodic Table:** The arrangement of elements in the periodic table has a symmetry that some scientists argue hints at an underlying intelligent design.

- **Faith and Scientific Inquiry:** Reconciling faith with science isn't merely a contemporary endeavor. Historical figures such as Gregor Mendel, a friar who founded modern genetics, epitomize the harmony between faith and reason.

- **Mathematical Universals:** The consistency of mathematical principles across the universe suggests an inherent order aligned with the concept of a Divine Creator.

In compiling this appendix, the goal has been to arm readers with a robust toolkit for navigating the intersecting realms of faith, science, and philosophy. Whether you are a scholar seeking rigorous academic engagement or a faithful believer looking for deeper understanding, the materials herein aim to enrich your journey toward the truth.

Glossary of Terms

This glossary aims to provide clear definitions and explanations for terms used throughout this book. Understanding these terms will help you grasp the intricate connections we make between faith, science, and philosophy to exalt the Roman Catholic Church and its divine origins.

- **Apologetics:** The branch of theology concerned with the defense and rational justification of Christianity.

- **Cosmology:** The science of the origin and development of the universe. In this book, it is also explored through theological lenses.

- **Divine Blueprint:** A metaphor for God's intricate design and plan for the universe, suggesting that every element and law of nature reflects divine intention.

- **Faith:** A profound trust and belief in God and the teachings of the Roman Catholic Church, often viewed as complementary to reason.

- **Intelligent Design:** The theory that the universe and living beings are the product of an intelligent cause rather than an undirected process such as natural selection.

- **Liturgical Calendar:** The annually recurring cycle of seasons and feasts observed in the Roman Catholic Church, marking significant events in the life of Jesus Christ and saints.

- **Natural Law:** A body of unchanging moral principles regarded as a basis for all human conduct, believed to be inherent through human nature and reflective of divine law.

- **Periodic Table:** A tabular arrangement of the chemical elements, ordered by their atomic number, electron configurations, and recurring chemical properties, seen here as evidence of divine order.

- **Philosophical Universals:** Core concepts and arguments in philosophy that suggest a universal truth or principle, often employed in arguments for the existence of God.

- **Proofs of Divine Origin:** Logical, empirical, and philosophical arguments and evidence presented to validate the belief that the Roman Catholic Church is of divine origin.

- **Reason:** The power of the mind to think, understand, and form judgments logically, viewed in this context as a tool that complements faith.

- **Systematic Theology:** The study of God and His relation to the world in a coherent and systematic way, often using a blend of scriptural and rational approaches.

- **Theological Implications:** Consequences or meanings derived from the study of God, often discussed in the context of scientific discoveries or philosophical arguments.

- **Universal Call:** The belief that all humans are invited and called to become part of the Roman Catholic Church, seen as God's true church.

Additional Resources

In the grand tapestry of our exploration through theology, philosophy, science, and the ultimate harmony they share, we've woven a comprehensive narrative that leads you to the inevitable conclusion: the Roman Catholic Church stands as God's chosen vessel. To further deepen your understanding and provide a multifaceted perspective, numerous additional resources can be invaluable. Here, I've compiled a curated list of books, articles, and other materials that span the various disciplines we've discussed. These resources will help you delve more deeply into each theme, offering a robust foundation for continued inquiry and reflection.

Theological Texts:

- *The Catechism of the Catholic Church* - This seminal work is essential for understanding the doctrines and teachings of the Roman Catholic Church. It provides a thorough introduction to the Church's stance on numerous theological issues, many of which are crucial to our discussions.

- *Summa Theologica* by St. Thomas Aquinas - A monumental work of theology and philosophy, it explores the nature of God, ethics, and the intersection of faith and reason. Aquinas' arguments for the existence of God and his understanding of divine order are foundational.

- *Mere Christianity* by C.S. Lewis - Though not a Roman Catholic text, Lewis' exploration of Christian beliefs offers profound insights into the rational basis for faith, complementing many of our earlier discussions on harmonizing science and religion.

- *The Everlasting Man* by G.K. Chesterton - This work provides a sweeping view of history through a Christian lens, arguing for the uniqueness and divinity of Jesus Christ. Chesterton's eloquence and erudition make complex theological arguments accessible.

Scientific Texts:

- *A Brief History of Time* by Stephen Hawking - This book delves into the mysteries of the universe, from the Big Bang to black holes. While Hawking's atheistic perspective contrasts with the theistic views presented in this book, understanding his arguments enriches the dialogue between science and religion.

- *The Structures of Scientific Revolutions* by Thomas Kuhn - Kuhn's exploration of paradigm shifts in science provides crucial context for understanding how scientific theories can be seen as part of a divine plan.

- *Cosmos* by Carl Sagan - Another secular perspective, yet essential for appreciating the vast, awe-inspiring complexity of the universe. Sagan's poetic description of the cosmos often evokes a sense of wonder that lends itself to theistic interpretation.

- *On the Origin of Species* by Charles Darwin - Darwin's seminal work on evolution. While some view it as a challenge to theistic belief, others see the mechanisms of evolution as part of God's creation.

Philosophical Texts:

- *The Republic* by Plato - Central to Western philosophy, Plato's dialogues explore justice, order, and the nature of reality. His Theory of Forms relates intriguingly to theological concepts of universals.

- *Critique of Pure Reason* by Immanuel Kant - Kant's examination of the limits and scope of human understanding is vital for appreciating the interplay between faith and reason.

- *Confessions* by St. Augustine - This autobiographical work is a stirring account of Augustine's conversion and his philosophical and theological reflections, providing a deep, personal insight into the journey of faith.

- *The Consolation of Philosophy* by Boethius - Written while Boethius faced execution, this text blends philosophical inquiry with

Christian theology, offering timeless meditations on fate and divine providence.

Mathematical and Cosmological Texts:

- *The Feynman Lectures on Physics* by Richard Feynman - A trilogy that brings physics alive while imparting a profound appreciation of the mathematical underpinnings of the universe. Feynman's insights resonate with the idea of a harmonious, divinely ordered cosmos.

- *Flatland: A Romance of Many Dimensions* by Edwin A. Abbott - This novella uses mathematical satire to explore dimensions and has been referenced in theological contexts for illustrating the limits of human perception of higher realities.

- *Principia Mathematica* by Alfred North Whitehead and Bertrand Russell - An ambitious work in mathematical logic that seeks to lay bare the logical foundations of mathematics, demonstrating a structure that many view as indicative of intelligent design.

- *A Mathematician's Apology* by G.H. Hardy - Hardy's reflections on the beauty and purity of mathematical thought underscore the divine elegance perceived in mathematical truths.

These resources serve as a bridge across the vast expanse of knowledge, linking the divine to the empirical, the sacred to the secular. By engaging with these texts, you're not just building upon what you've learned but also inviting new dialogues and perspectives into your understanding. Remember, the quest for truth is not confined to a single discipline; it is multifaceted, continuous, and deeply interwoven with our existence. Dive into these works with an open mind and a reflective heart, and may your journey lead you ever closer to the divine harmony we all seek.

THE 15 PRAYERS OF ST. BRIDGET

 These Prayers and these Promises have been copied from a book printed in Toulouse in 1740 and published by the P. Adrien Parvilliers of the Company of Jesus, Apostolic Missionary of the Holy Land, with approbation, permission and recommendation to distribute them.
Pope Pius IX took cognisance of these Prayers with the prologue; he approved them May 31, 1862, recognising them as true and for the good of souls.

As St. Bridget for a long time wanted to know the number of blows Our Lord received during His Passion, He one day appeared to her and said: "I received 5480 blows on My Body. If you wish to honour them in some way, say 15 Our Fathers and 15 Hail Marys with the following Prayers (which He taught her) for a whole year. When the year is up, you will have honoured each one of My Wounds."

He made the following promises to anyone who recited these Prayers for a whole year:

1. I will deliver 15 souls of his lineage from Purgatory.
2. 15 souls of his lineage will be confirmed and preserved in grace.
3. 15 sinners of his lineage will be converted.
4. Whoever recites these Prayers will attain the first degree of perfection.
5. 15 days before his death I will give him My Precious Body in order that he may escape eternal starvation; I will give him My Precious Blood to drink lest he thirst eternally.

6. 15 days before his death he will feel a deep contrition for all his sins and will have a perfect knowledge of them.
7. I will place before him the sign of My Victorious Cross for his help and defence against the attacks of his enemies.
8. Before his death I shall come with My Dearest Beloved Mother.
9. I shall graciously receive his soul, and will lead it into eternal joys.
10. And having led it there I shall give him a special draught from the fountain of My Deity, something I will not for those who have not recited My Prayers.
11. Let it be known that whoever may have been living in a state of mortal sin for 30 years, but who will recite devoutly, or have the intention to recite these Prayers, the Lord will forgive him all his sins.
12. I shall protect him from strong temptations.
13. I shall preserve and guard his 5 senses.
14. I shall preserve him from a sudden death.
15. His soul will be delivered from eternal death.
16. He will obtain all he asks for from God and the Blessed Virgin.
17. If he has lived all his life doing his own will and he is to die the next day, his life will be prolonged.
18. Every time one recites these Prayers he gains 100 days indulgence.
19. He is assured of being joined to the supreme Choir of Angels.
20. Whoever teaches these Prayers to another, will have continuous joy and merit which will endure eternally.
21. There where these Prayers are being said or will be said in the future God is present with His grace.

Each prayer is preceded by one Our Father and one

Hail Mary.

Our Father, who art in heaven, hallowed be thy name.
Thy kingdom come.
Thy will be done on earth as it is in heaven.
Give us this day our daily bread and forgive us our
trespasses as we forgive those who trespass against us and
lead us not into temptation but deliver us from evil. **Amen**

Hail Mary, full of grace, the Lord is with thee; blessed art
thou among women and blessed is the fruit of thy womb,
Jesus.
Holy Mary, Mother of God, pray for us sinners, now and at
the hour of our death. **Amen.**

FIRST PRAYER
Our Father – Hail Mary.
O Jesus Christ! Eternal Sweetness to those who love Thee,
joy surpassing all joy and all desire, Salvation and Hope of
all sinners, Who hast proved that Thou hast no greater
desire than to be among men, even assuming human nature
at the fullness of time for the love of men, recall all the
sufferings Thou hast endured from the instant of Thy
conception, and especially during Thy Passion, as it was
decreed and ordained from all eternity in the Divine plan.

Remember, O Lord, that during the Last Supper with Thy
disciples, having washed their feet, Thou gavest them Thy
Most Precious Body and Blood, and while at the same time
thou didst sweetly console them, Thou didst foretell them
Thy coming Passion.
Remember the sadness and bitterness which Thou didst
experience in Thy Soul as Thou Thyself bore witness saying:
"My Soul is sorrowful even unto death."

Remember all the fear, anguish and pain that Thou didst
suffer in Thy delicate Body before the torment of the
Crucifixion, when, after having prayed three times, bathed

in a sweat of blood, Thou wast betrayed by Judas, Thy disciple, arrested by the people of a nation Thou hadst chosen and elevated, accused by false witnesses, unjustly judged by three judges during the flower of Thy youth and during the solemn Paschal season.

Remember that Thou wast despoiled of Thy garments and clothed in those of derision; that Thy Face and Eyes were veiled, that Thou wast buffeted, crowned with thorns, a reed placed in Thy Hands, that Thou was crushed with blows and overwhelmed with affronts and outrages.
In memory of all these pains and sufferings which Thou didst endure before Thy Passion on the Cross, grant me before my death true contrition, a sincere and entire confession, worthy satisfaction and the remission of all my sins. **Amen.**

SECOND PRAYER
Our Father – Hail Mary.
O Jesus! True liberty of angels, Paradise of delights, remember the horror and sadness which Thou didst endure when Thy enemies, like furious lions, surrounded Thee, and by thousands of insults, spits, blows, lacerations and other unheard-of-cruelties, tormented Thee at will.

In consideration of these torments and insulting words, I beseech Thee, O my Saviour, to deliver me from all my enemies, visible and invisible, and to bring me, under Thy protection, to the perfection of eternal salvation. **Amen.**

THIRD PRAYER
Our Father – Hail Mary.
O Jesus! Creator of Heaven and earth Whom nothing can encompass or limit, Thou Who dost enfold and hold all under Thy Loving power, remember the very bitter pain.

Thou didst suffer when the Jews nailed Thy Sacred Hands

and Feet to the Cross by blow after blow with big blunt nails, and not finding Thee in a pitiable enough state to satisfy their rage, they enlarged Thy Wounds, and added pain to pain, and with indescribable cruelty stretched Thy Body on the Cross, pulled Thee from all sides, thus dislocating Thy Limbs.

I beg of Thee, O Jesus, by the memory of this most Loving suffering of the Cross, to grant me the grace to fear Thee and to Love Thee. **Amen.**

FOURTH PRAYER
Our Father - Hail Mary.
O Jesus! Heavenly Physician, raised aloft on the Cross to heal our wounds with Thine, remember the bruises which Thou didst suffer and the weakness of all Thy Members which were distended to such a degree that never was there pain like unto Thine.

From the crown of Thy Head to the Soles of Thy Feet there was not one spot on Thy Body that was not in torment, and yet, forgetting all Thy sufferings, Thou didst not cease to pray to Thy Heavenly Father for Thy enemies, saying: "Father forgive them for they know not what they do."

Through this great Mercy, and in memory of this suffering, grant that the remembrance of Thy Most Bitter Passion may effect in us a perfect contrition and the remission of all our sins. **Amen.**

FIFTH PRAYER
Our Father - Hail Mary.
O Jesus! Mirror of eternal splendour, remember the sadness which Thou experienced, when contemplating in the light of Thy Divinity the predestination of those who would be saved by the merits of Thy Sacred Passion.

Thou didst see at the same time, the great multitude of reprobates who would be damned for their sins, and Thou didst complain bitterly of those hopeless lost and unfortunate sinners.

Through this abyss of compassion and pity, and especially through the goodness which Thou displayed to the good thief when Thou saidst to him: "This day, thou shalt be with Me in Paradise." I beg of Thee, O Sweet Jesus, that at the hour of my death, Thou wilt show me mercy. **Amen**.

SIXTH PRAYER
Our Father - Hail Mary.
O Jesus! Beloved and most desirable King, remember the grief Thou didst suffer, when naked and like a common criminal.

Thou was fastened and raised on the Cross, when all Thy relatives and friends abandoned Thee, except Thy Beloved Mother, who remained close to Thee during Thy agony and whom Thou didst entrust to Thy faithful disciple when Thou saidst to Mary: "Woman, behold thy son!" and to St. John: "Son, behold thy Mother!"

I beg of Thee O my Saviour, by the sword of sorrow which pierced the soul of Thy holy Mother, to have compassion on me in all my affliction and tribulations, both corporal and spiritual, and to assist me in all my trials, and especially at the hour of my death. **Amen**.

SEVENTH PRAYER
Our Father - Hail Mary.
O Jesus! Inexhaustible Fountain of compassion, Who by a profound gesture of Love, said from the Cross: "I thirst!" suffered from the thirst for the salvation of the human race.

I beg of Thee O my Saviour, to inflame in our hearts the desire to tend toward perfection in all our acts; and to extinguish in us the concupiscence of the flesh and the ardor of worldly desires. **Amen**.

EIGHTH PRAYER
Our Father - Hail Mary.
O Jesus! Sweetness of hearts, delight of the spirit, by the bitterness of the vinegar and gall which Thou didst taste on the Cross for Love of us, grant us the grace to receive worthily.

Thy Precious Body and Blood during our life and at the hour of our death, that they may serve as a remedy and consolation for our souls. **Amen.**

NINTH PRAYER
Our Father - Hail Mary.
O Jesus! Royal virtue, joy of the mind, recall the pain Thou didst endure when, plunged in an ocean of bitterness at the approach of death, insulted, outraged by the Jews.

Thou didst cry out in a loud voice that Thou was abandoned by Thy Father, saying: "My God, My God, why hast Thou forsaken me?"

Through this anguish, I beg of Thee, O my Saviour, not to abandon me in the terrors and pains of my death. **Amen.**

TENTH PRAYER
Our Father - Hail Mary.
O Jesus! Who art the beginning and end of all things, life and virtue, remembers that for our sakes Thou was plunged in an abyss of suffering from the soles of Thy Feet to the crown

of Thy Head.

In consideration of the enormity of Thy Wounds, teach me to keep, through pure love, Thy Commandments, whose way is wide and easy for those who love Thee. **Amen.**

ELEVENTH PRAYER
Our Father - Hail Mary.
O Jesus! Deep abyss of mercy, I beg of Thee, in memory of Thy Wounds which penetrated to the very marrow of Thy Bones and to the depth of Thy being, to draw me, a miserable sinner, overwhelmed by my offenses, away from sin and to hide me from Thy Face justly irritated against me, hide me in Thy wounds, until Thy anger and just indignation shall have passed away. **Amen.**

TWELFTH PRAYER
Our Father - Hail Mary.
O Jesus! Mirror of Truth, symbol of unity, bond of charity, remember the multitude of wounds with which Thou wast afflicted from head to foot, torn and reddened by the spilling of Thy adorable Blood. O great and universal pain, which Thou didst suffer in Thy virginal flesh for love of us! Sweetest Jesus! What is there that Thou couldst have done for us which Thou has not done!

May the fruit of Thy suffering be renewed in my soul by the faithful remembrance of Thy Passion, and may Thy love increase in my heart each day, until I see Thee in eternity: Thou Who art the treasure of every real good and every joy, which I beg Thee to grant me, O Sweetest Jesus, in heaven. **Amen.**

THIRTEENTH PRAYER
Our Father - Hail Mary.

O Jesus! Strong Lion, Immortal and Invincible King, remember the pain which Thou didst endure when all Thy strength, both moral and physical, was entirely exhausted, Thou didst bow Thy Head, saying: "It is consummated!"

Through this anguish and grief, I beg of Thee Lord Jesus, to have mercy on me at the hour of my death when my mind will be greatly troubled and my soul will be in anguish. **Amen.**

FOURTEENTH PRAYER
Our Father – Hail Mary.
O Jesus! Only Son of the Father, Splendour and Figure of His Substance, remember the simple and humble recommendation.

Thou didst make of Thy Soul to Thy Eternal Father, saying: "Father, into Thy Hands I commend My Spirit!" And with Thy Body all torn, and Thy Heart Broken, and the bowels of Thy Mercy open to redeem us, Thou didst Expire.

By this Precious Death, I beg of Thee O King of Saints, comfort me and help me to resist the devil, the flesh and the world, so that being dead to the world I may live for Thee alone.

I beg of Thee at the hour of my death to receive me, a pilgrim and an exile returning to Thee. **Amen.**

FIFTEENTH PRAYER
Our Father – Hail Mary.
O Jesus! True and fruitful Vine! Remember the abundant outpouring of Blood which Thou didst so generously shed from Thy Sacred Body as juice from grapes in a wine press.

From Thy Side, pierced with a lance by a soldier, blood and

water issued forth until there was not left in Thy Body a single drop, and finally, like a bundle of myrrh lifted to the top of the Cross Thy delicate Flesh was destroyed, the very Substance of Thy Body withered, and the Marrow of Thy Bones dried up.

Through this bitter Passion and through the outpouring of Thy Precious Blood, I beg of Thee, O Sweet Jesus, to receive my soul when I am in my death agony. **Amen.**

CONCLUSION
O Sweet Jesus! Pierce my heart so that my tears of penitence and love will be my bread day and night; may I be converted entirely to Thee, may my heart be Thy perpetual habitation, may my conversation be pleasing to Thee, and may the end of my life be so praiseworthy that I may merit Heaven and there with Thy saints, praise Thee forever. **Amen.**